Lawrence S. Munson

How to Conduct Training Seminars

Lawrence S. Munson

How to Conduct Training Seminars

McGRAW-HILL BOOK COMPANY

New York   St. Louis   San Francisco   London

Montreal   Paris   Sydney   Tokyo   Toronto

Bonnie Binkert and Michael Hennelly were the editors of this book. Al Cetta was the
designer. Reiko Okamura supervised the production. It was set in Gael by Kingsport
Press, Inc.

Printed and bound by R. R. Donnelley and Sons, Inc.

Library of Congress Cataloging in Publication Data

Munson, Lawrence S.
  How to conduct training seminars.

  Includes index.
  1. Executives—Training of. 2. Seminars. I. Title.
HF5549.5.T7M86 1984   658.4'07124   83–11318
ISBN 0-07-044051-4
1 2 3 4 5 6 7 8 9 DOC/DOC 8 9 8 7 6 5 4

ISBN 0-07-044051-4

To Gretchen

Contents

Chapter 5: Developing the Training Plan 62

**Chapter 8:   Getting the Most Out of Your Seminar
    Leaders**   117

Preface

Training seminars can be enjoyable—and they can really pay off. They can also be an agony of boredom, frustration, and wasted time. As I was reflecting on this thought one evening, it occurred to me that a great deal of experience has been gained by those of us who use management training seminars and workshops as a primary means for helping our clients improve their management systems and effect basic change in their management practices. In this book, I want to share this experience with others. In particular, I want to reach training directors and those executives responsible for developing human resources in all types of organizations. On balance, most things have been done right, but I have had to learn from my mistakes just like everyone else. Many of these mistakes are cited in the pages of this book. They tend to be more entertaining and sometimes more instructive than the triumphs.

Getting back to the point, training seminars can and should be exciting. They almost *have* to be if we want to get commitment to put new knowledge to work on the job. And that's where they pay off—on the job. Have you ever participated in a fast-moving seminar with a high level of stimulating interplay among alert, informed participants? If you have, you know that seminars, potentially, can hold your intense interest just as much as a good mystery novel or a finely tuned Broadway who-done-it.

If you are a student of people, you can almost always find a challenging assortment in a training seminar. At first, they are rather indistinguishable from each other except as to physical features and dress. Then slowly individual characters emerge as we learn about the backgrounds they come from and observe their behavior in the group. There are those who have to dominate and seek leadership roles. There are the fun-lovers who create enjoyment for themselves and others. This type can often get people in trouble at night, whooping it up enjoying the freedom from home responsibilities and the fellowship of new friends. There are the quietly critical, the introverts, the insecure. Here is a father image. There is a militant feminist. What may not be obvious to the participants is that staging an effective, stimulating seminar is no accident. It requires the right organizational climate, an appropriate setting, and very careful planning. Without these, the most skilled seminar leader cannot succeed. Follow-up after the seminar is also necessary, if we want to succeed in improving performance on the job, which is the basic reason for it all.

The material collected in this book follows a natural sequence. After an introductory chapter, the next seven chapters are concerned with all the things that have to take place in advance of the seminar. Chapters nine and ten deal with the conduct of the seminar itself. And the last two chapters review follow-up techniques after the seminar and present an overall summary. Where appropriate, checklists, diagrams, and examples useful to training directors and seminar leaders have been included with the text.

Let me here acknowledge that this book has become possible through the contributions of a large number of experienced professionals. It is based more on the direct inputs of experienced practitioners than it is upon library research. It has more by way of anecdote than statistical tables. Many of the people I have drawn upon are from the consulting firms with which I have been associated. Their ideas and experience have proven to be a rich source of material for the chapters that follow. Let me also thank the many training directors who gave their time to discuss the matters contained in this book. While that list is too long to reproduce here, their help has been considerable. Also, Elizabeth Koppelman, thanks for your seemingly endless hours of typing and your editorial suggestions.

Lawrence S. Munson

How to Conduct Training Seminars

Chapter 1

The Growing Importance of Training Seminars

The huge and increasing amounts of money being spent on formal, off-the-job training of employees in all kinds of organized endeavors raises a question that has never been satisfactorily answered: are we getting our money's worth? Are we getting the improvement in the productivity of our human resources that has to be the ultimate aim of any training program? Estimates on the total dollars spent are in the billions and growing. The American Society for Training and Development puts the total U.S.A./Canadian market somewhere between $30 billion and $40 billion.* Hope Reports, Inc. estimates that the market has more than doubled between 1977 and 1981.*

To be sure, not all of this money is being invested in training seminars. But the large number of training directors we have contacted on this point agree without exception that the training seminar or workshop is the "workhorse" of the training function.

Such a massive outlay for employee training may well be the reflection of a deep concern about the productivity of human resources. Though criticisms have been made on the methodology, statistics on productivity in recent years seem to indicate that an adverse trend

* These estimates were provided by Hope Reports, Inc., Rochester, N.Y. in a seminar they conducted, May 20, 1982, in Rochester, N.Y.

has set in. Statistics on productivity are too often and persistently unfavorable. Challenges to traditional U.S. concepts on managing human resources appear in a stream of articles and speeches. It would certainly appear timely to consider how to improve the cost effectiveness of the huge number of training seminars that are being conducted across the country every year.

RATIONALE

The rationale for this enormous investment in formal training is simple. There is a widespread need in business, industry, government, and institutions of all kinds to make people more productive and to make people in new jobs more quickly productive. Natural talent gets people only so far. Consider the youngster learning to play the piano. Given considerable ability, it may be possible for the child to learn "by ear." But every teacher, every parent knows that natural talent alone cannot make a concert pianist. To become a professional pianist requires a great commitment to training and practice. Then again, with the spread of technological progress, there are very few jobs where natural talent will even get you started. The need for specialized knowledge and skills is virtually omnipresent.

Shortening the time it takes for new employees to become productive can provide a very real pay-off. If new sales representatives can be out in the field selling effectively two weeks earlier through improved training, it can be directly translatable into added sales revenue and profit. The same is true for a host of jobs: word processing, machine tooling, operating a computer, programming for computers, telephone switchboard operation. Even positions requiring advanced university degrees such as in business administration, medicine and law, still require some training in the specifics of the particular job.

Training in management skills presents a special need, although it is not as universally recognized as the need for technical training. It is well known that the instinctive approaches most people take when they become managers are not going to be effective in the long run. As Louis Allen pointed out twenty-five years ago,* most people who are thrust into management positions will tend to be indifferent to the needs of the individuals in the group being managed. They tend to keep all the important decision-making to themselves, without soliciting or listening to the ideas of others. They act intuitively and spontaneously, without taking the time to gather and analyze facts, or time

* Louis A. Allen, *Management and Organization*, McGraw-Hill Book Company, New York, 1958, pp 5–8.

to consider alternatives. They organize around people instead of around the work to be done. They poke their noses continuously into the work of their subordinates. They personally check up to make sure everything is going right. All these characteristics tend to create an environment, in more mature organizations, that stifles individual creativity and prevents full job satisfaction. Managers have to be trained away from these instinctive approaches and toward methods that are far more likely to be effective in raising the productivity of human resources.

TRAINING VEHICLES

Not all training is done through seminars, which can be defined as any organized, group learning experience with a high degree of participation and interaction within the group, which varies in size from seven or eight to 30 in number. The term includes "workshops," which can be viewed as a kind of seminar with an especially high proportion of individual work exercises and skill-building. There are other training vehicles that contribute in their way to improving human knowledge, attitudes and skills. Each has its appropriate place.

Coaching

The most effective training is done on the job—the direct coaching of subordinate by superior. Because the two are in more or less constant contact in the workplace, this person-to-person teaching offers a more continuing and intensive opportunity to change behavior. The very nature of the relationship makes the subordinate receptive to the guidance of the superior. A surprisingly high proportion of the most successful executives in the country can point to the positive assistance provided by some interested and able senior manager in the course of their careers.

Lectures

Lectures are not often used for employee training. Their widespread use in our universities is due, no doubt, to the large number of students per faculty member—at least in the basic or survey courses. Although lectures appear on the surface to be a way of reaching large numbers of people efficiently, the lack of opportunity for participation impedes learning and encourages mind-wandering—a particular concern for employer-initiated training where the participants' attendance is a requirement imposed by the employer and not a self-generated interest in the subject matter.

Some teachers have found ways to depart from straight lecture to maintain a high level of attention and some involvement even in large audiences. One technique is to divide the large group into smaller groups to discuss and reach conclusions on some subject with subsequent reports back to the whole group. Another method, which may be more practical in large classrooms, is to pit one side of the room against the other on some issue that will generate interest. But it is not always easy to use these techniques because of sheer numbers, or because of the practical difficulties of dividing into sub-groups.

Informal Discussion Groups

From time to time groups are formed, or form themselves to exchange ideas and experience. At McKinsey & Company it used to be the practice (and may still be) at the conclusion of a client assignment for the team of consultants who worked together on it to get together and ask themselves: what would they have done differently were they to have the chance to do the assignment over again? It proved to be a valuable learning process. The debriefing was not obligatory. It was simply a useful practice that developed. Students in our universities frequently form up into study groups for the same purpose. They have learned that reading assigned text material is not enough. They have to analyze and react to it. Posing questions and challenges to each other helps them all reach deeper levels of understanding—often resulting in a mature critique rather than an unquestioning acceptance of the assigned text material.

Self-Development

Some people have a great capacity for learning through reading and observing, strictly on their own. Self-development is becoming a much more important training vehicle in recent years with computer-assisted instruction, and with videotape and video disc equipment. The expense of the equipment and software can sometimes be justified by the large numbers of people to be trained. The cost per person is greatly reduced and the impact on the individual can be extremely high.

Projects

A further means for acquiring new knowledge and skills is through participation in projects. The range and importance of projects assigned to newer members of general-line consulting firms, such as McKinsey & Company, Booz Allen & Hamilton or Arthur D. Little, undoubtedly accounts for much of their success in training and developing their own professional staff. Their professional people are said to get five years' experience in their first two years.

The range of available subject matter for projects is very large. It is limited only by the resourcefulness of the training director or line manager involved. Here are a few examples: developing a training manual; researching and reporting on some specific subject of importance; conducting a training program; or improving a procedure or process.

THE TRAINING SEMINAR

Seminars are the most widely used of all the available vehicles for employee training. American Management Associations alone puts on 3,000 seminars each year. Our own firm will conduct roughly 1,000 seminars per year, worldwide, half of which will be in the U.S.A. Add to these numbers the activities of literally thousands of other organizations and individuals conducting or sponsoring training seminars throughout the country. The total seminar activity is huge.

Advantages

There are some practical advantages that account for this widespread use of seminars. They are quite efficient in terms of per capita cost; they are easily adaptable to different participant groups; and they can be very effective in terms of impact. Furthermore, there is a large number of good programs available that save training directors the time, cost and effort required to develop their own programs.

Efficiency. Seminars can reach large populations with common needs quite efficiently. They can be quite tightly structured around standard audio/visuals so that a number of different trainers can deliver essentially the same subject matter to widely separated groups. Union Carbide Corporation, for example, sends its trainers into dozens of different countries around the world to conduct management training seminars. They are teaching new managers the Union Carbide Management System so that all over the world the Company's managers will have a common management philosophy and common approaches to such management fundamentals as developing objectives, establishing standards of performance, and action planning.

The principal advantage of seminars over on-the-job coaching is the ability to reach twenty to twenty-five people—sometimes even larger groups—at the same time. By frequently breaking up into smaller subgroups, the opportunity for involvement and interaction is greatly increased, which adds to the seminar's effectiveness. If seminars are designed properly, and conducted by able discussion leaders, groups of up to twenty-five participants can be reached very easily, at one and the same time. Lectures can reach substantially larger audiences. But as the audiences get larger, the opportunity for interaction between trainer and trainee, and among trainees lessens. The considerable experience represented in any audience cannot be usefully presented and shared in a lecture setting.

Adaptability. Almost any subject can be taught in a seminar format. The subject can be very broad, such as a comprehensive course in management concepts and methods. Or it can be very narrow, such as how to operate a specific piece of equipment, like a new word processor. Then again, essentially the same subject matter can be oriented by a skilled discussion leader to the needs and interests of different groups. In fact, this happens almost inevitably. The questions raised by participants and the experiences they share provide for this adaptation almost without conscious effort on the part of the trainer.

High Impact Potential. The training seminar also has the potential for getting a high level of participant commitment and motivation, primarily because of its emphasis on participant involvement and interaction. As this happens within any participant group, there is a group-induced mutual reinforcement that adds to the impact value. This high impact potential is the seminar's principal advantage over lectures and self-instruction. It is a truly unusual person who can "psyche" himself or herself up listening to a lecture or reading a textbook.

Availability of Proven Programs. Training directors know only too well that there is a thriving industry that develops and sells them training seminars. They know because they are continuously subjected to aggressive selling efforts. Some of these programs are conducted by the vendor. Others are run by in-house trainers trained by the vendor. But the point is, a wide range of good quality programs *is* available. Surveys have indicated that vendors located in the U.S.A. alone had revenues of $1.5 billion in 1981 from selling off-the-shelf programs, standard seminars and custom-designed programs.*

* Hope Reports, Inc. Seminar, "The U.S. Training Business," Rochester, N.Y., May 20, 1982.

Limitations

Training seminars have disadvantages or limitations as well as advantages. Just like all those stories that used to be passed around, there is "bad news" as well as "good news." But these limitations can be avoided or lessened by careful planning.

Limited Skill Building. Seminars are often ineffective in building skills, i.e., forming new behavior patterns. The constraints of time and the participant-to-instructor ratio make it difficult to get individual participants trained in new skills. Participants will acquire knowledge and may generate favorable attitudes, but typically skill-building is left to on-the-job application. This limitation is less true for "workshops," that are designed to have a substantial portion of individual work exercises, role-playing or behavior modeling.

In management seminars, for example, role-playing with group critiques can provide some skill-building in interviewing, communicating, and performance counseling. Likewise, individual work exercises with group critiques can at least start the behavior change process in regard to developing objectives, standards of performance, and action planning.

Leader Dependence. The importance of the discussion leader to the success of a training seminar can be another disadvantage, or is at least a risk. No matter how good the basic design, any training program needs the perceptivity and resourcefulness of the leader to draw out the participants and generate the most stimulating group discussion. The importance of the leader lessens as the seminar structure is tightened. A 2-hour program in supervisory skills with taped narration, 160 synchronized 35mm slides, and detailed participant workbook will be only slightly leader dependent. But even here, a poor leader can make the program ineffective.

Needs Matching. There has to be a good match between the needs and expectations of the participants and the subject matter of the program, or else the seminar will be ineffective. Some years ago, I was made uncomfortably aware of this limitation. I was conducting a program for third-level managers at the corporate education center of a prominent multi-billion dollar manufacturer. Two days into the program I had an active participant rebellion on my hands. Under the leadership of two very attractive, articulate sales types, who went behind my back to the training director sponsoring the program, the group said, in effect, "This doesn't meet our needs!" They were referring in particular to an in-depth workshop portion of the program on developing standards of performance. It turned out that only three participants in the class had even read the short write-up on the course in the company's brochure. Those three were supportive, because the write-up clearly indicated that emphasis would be placed on developing standards of performance. (Furthermore, I might add, the course was carefully designed in response to an extensive needs analysis.)

Cost. A final limitation is cost. The full cost is almost always hidden. Sometimes the only costs that show up in the training director's budget are professional fees to consultants, costs of educational materials and, perhaps, the cost of the facility. Usually much larger are the transportation and subsistence expenses of the seminar participants; and still larger, the economic cost entailed in being away from the job. Nevertheless, on balance all these limitations are more than counterbalanced by the advantages of the seminar vehicle.

THE CHALLENGE PRESENTED

Given the dominance of the training seminar as a means for improving the productivity of your human resources, how can you make sure you are using it most effectively? What can you do to make sure your investment in training seminars is really paying off? The remaining chapters of this book seek to provide some answers.

Chapter 2

The Organization Environment

Any account of training seminars has to start with the organizational climate in which they take place. At one extreme is a surprisingly large number of companies which have no formal training function. At the other extreme are companies that place an extraordinarily high priority on formal training. Many of these companies have established in-house education centers with highly qualified staffs to provide a wide range of training programs.

Most frequently, training directors* are presented with an organizational climate. In the short-term they have little influence over it. The situation is faced by all training directors who are brought into the training function from somewhere else in the company or from the outside. Over a period of time, however, there are some things they can do if they analyze the various groups influencing the internal value system and make some effort to change the attitudes of these groups.

---

* "Training director" is a term I'll use to refer to an individual responsible for the training and development of human resources regardless of exact title.

IMPORTANCE OF THE "CLIMATE"

To illustrate the significance of organizational environment, assume that Harry and Joan come back from a four-day management training seminar full of ideas and enthusiasm. They've taken essentially the same course, but at different times and under different circumstances. Let's take Harry first. Harry goes to a seminar conducted by an accomplished outside consultant and is very impressed. When he returns, he calls a meeting with his staff. He tries to teach them in twenty minutes what he learned over the entire four days of the seminar. His people listen politely. Some even show enthusiasm. But below the surface, Harry's announced intention to "start doing things differently around here" meets a wall of quiet but determined opposition. Two weeks later, Harry is back in his old routine. His seminar workbook is displayed proudly on the bookshelf—gathering dust.

Now let us see what happens to Joan. Her seminar had the same basic subject matter, same educational design, and an equally accomplished discussion leader. But it was set in quite a different organizational environment. A group of twenty managers with roughly equivalent management experience gathered together in the seminar room with some positive expectations. They had heard good things about the program from bosses and peers who had already been through it. As they settle down in their places, the president of the company comes in and says to them:

"Welcome to our seminar on professional management methods. I think you'll get a lot out of it. I know I did when I went through with the first group, which consisted of all the senior officers in the company. The program has been adapted from a standard management training program to meet our specific needs, including the incorporation of some of our own terminology.

"Some of the most important parts of the program are being built into our company's established planning and performance appraisal practices. I'm referring specifically to mission statements with standards of performance; also 'Action Planning' and integration of performance appraisals with the planning process. You will be able to apply these aspects of the program on the job when you finish the seminar.

"Don't misunderstand me. We don't want you to fit tightly into a carefully defined mold. We value individual creativity and recognize that individual styles may, and perhaps should, differ. But if we all use the same vocabulary and certain common management processes, we can be much more effective as a team."

Needless to say, Joan and the other participants in the second group showed significantly greater commitment during the seminar and now demonstrate clearly identifiable behavior change on the job. It needs to be footnoted that this particular president sets a living example of a professional manager. He means what he said. And he practices what he preached.

The example makes the point. Harry probably gained some useful knowledge. But he showed little if any improved management performance on the job. Even the knowledge he gained will be gradually lost through lack of use. Joan probably absorbed the same amount of knowledge as Harry. But, unlike Harry, she did change her behavior patterns on the job—she put this knowledge to work and kept it as part of her on-going knowledge inventory. In this illustration, the president of the company established the importance of the training seminar, helped create favorable attitudes on the part of the participants, and influenced the group norms that would be working on the participants when they returned to their jobs.

The organizational influences on training function can be usefully considered in terms of three groups: (1) top management; (2) the immediate superiors of seminar participants; and (3) their peers. "Top management" doesn't necessarily mean the chief executive officer and his or her immediate staff. It is a convenient term to describe any highly placed authoritative group of executives heading up a reasonably autonomous organization component. The immediate superiors of the participants in any seminar is a population that changes with each seminar. But it is convenient to identify this group separately because of the important influence of the immediate superiors on the post seminar behavior of the participants. The peer group is made up of fellow employees, neither superior nor subordinates, with whom the participants associate in a working relationship on the job. It includes the other participants in every seminar group.

TOP MANAGEMENT INFLUENCES

Of all these three groups, top management has the greatest influence on organizational environment. Top management is the power center for deciding whether there should be a training function at all. In some organizations the training function is a heritage from past management and is given little direction and support by the present top management group. Then again, there are companies that make major investments each year in the training and development of their human resources: companies that integrate the training function into their overall system of management; companies whose chief executives take an active and visible role in the training function.

Budgetary Support

The budgetary support provided by top management determines the very existence of a formal training function. Practices vary widely in this respect. At one extreme are companies like General Electric and Western Electric who have established large, well-equipped corporate education centers whose very existence establishes the importance of the function. Merrill Lynch & Company, for another example, has dedicated a whole floor of its corporate headquarters on Liberty Plaza in New York City to the training function. At the other extreme are companies, sometimes companies of substantial size, who don't recognize the function at all.

Most companies fall somewhere between these two extremes. One of them I remember well is a very fast-growing computer company in Massachusetts. This company has a small, constantly changing training staff and apparently a very modest budget. Presumably to make their few dollars go farther, they always chose unusual, out-of-the-way locations for their seminars. One of the places they selected was a charming old Inn in FitzWilliam, New Hampshire. Notwithstanding its historic ambience, it was a poor place to hold seminars.

One cold February morning, at about 6:30 A.M., I was proudly shown the seminar room by the proprietor. I had been unable to find him to show me the room the night before because he had gone to bed early. What he showed me was an outside porch that had been walled in with some inexpensive, removable plastic panels. The floor creaked a bit and was not uniformly level. Some lights had been strung around the ceiling for purposes of illumination, purposes which they served only dimly. But the main problem was the cold, which the electric space heaters could not overcome. You could see your own breath. It took only a very few minutes for the cold to clamp itself tightly around your limbs. As the only available option to this inadequate room, my seminar group ended up in the living room, near a modernized wood-burning Franklin stove, which needed frequent attention. With workbooks in lap, and the easel nestled in the curve of a vintage grand piano, we all gallantly launched into our seminar on professional management concepts and practices.

Naturally, budgetary support in itself does not alone provide for the right organizational environment. But it is an essential starting point. Without funding there can be no training function. With inadequate funding, it cannot have a significant impact.

Management Practices

The kind of management practices established by top management represents the second way that top management influences the environment within which formal training takes place. Sometimes there is a very direct relationship. For example, if top management introduces a management system involving the cascading of objectives and use of standards of performance, managers have to be taught how to use the system. Similarly, if a new performance appraisal and performance counseling system is installed, it almost necessarily has to be implemented through training. The same is true if top management decides a new emphasis is to be given to on-the-job coaching. In all these cases, participants in the training seminars know they will be expected to put their new knowledge to work on the job. This expectation gives them a strong sense of commitment which helps make the seminar effective.

At other times the influence of top management may be indirect, but nevertheless important. For example, if organizational policy requires that performance appraisals of managers specifically include an evaluation of their performance in training and developing people, it helps to give formal training a higher level of importance to all concerned. If top management supports career planning and management development programs that require the successful completion of certain training courses, it necessarily creates a demand for those courses.

Public Manifestations

A third way top management helps is through public manifestations of support. These can be in the annual report, in company publications of various kinds, or at meetings. Top management support can also take the form of personal attendance at training sessions. For example, Paul Sticht, Chairman of R. J. Reynolds Inc., attended a dinner held before the start of a series of top-down management training seminars for a subsidiary, Sea-Land Service, Inc. He didn't say a great deal. But he was there—which added significantly to the importance of the occasion. Joseph Dionne, President of McGraw-Hill Inc., and James C. Corcoran, Chairman of General Accident and Indemnity, use this approach too, with similar effectiveness.

Serving as a Behavior Model

The fourth means, top management serving as a behavior model, applies most appropriately to management training seminars. The model can be either supportive or nonsupportive. If, as in the illustration at the start of this chapter, top management conducts itself in accordance with the generally accepted concepts of professional management, it can be a real plus. If the chief executive is a good delegator, insists on completed work, creates a favorable motivational climate and does all the other "good things" taught in management courses, the rest of the management population will most probably do so, too.

It is strange, in a way, to reflect upon the influence of the top team, especially the chief executive, as a behavior model. For example, a very conservative, old-line insurance company in Philadelphia got a new president. He came from another company. Much to the astonishment of the management bureaucracy, conservatively clad day after day for years in white shirts and dark suits, the new president was observed wearing a *yellow* shirt on two separate occasions within the first two weeks of his regime! Within three weeks, I am told on good authority, all the men's clothing stores in downtown Philadelphia were sold out of yellow shirts!

The point is that the top management behavior model can be an important influence on behavior, an influence that can in some situations be negative. To give an example, the president of a large, East coast electric utility system was the type that had to be involved in and have knowledge of all operations. He was the first to arrive in the office every morning, using this opportunity to scan and sort all the incoming mail. He would also telephone the superintendants of each of the major generating plants daily to get up-dated on all operating conditions. In doing so, he effectively by-passed intermediate management levels, undermining their effectiveness and motivation. It is no wonder that he had little time left to think more broadly about strategic planning and upgrading the effectiveness of human resources at all levels. Quite understandably, his management style was emulated by managers at successively lower management levels throughout the system, creating an environment that discouraged any training and development in modern professional management methods.

Direct Involvement

The fifth vehicle of impact for top management is direct involvement. When Union Carbide Corporation went through a massive management training effort from top to bottom as part of a major restructuring of management processes, the company's top management was directly involved. At every seminar held at their facility in Tarrytown, New York, one of the four top executives in the Company would start off the first day. He would welcome the group, explain the background leading up to the program, and stress its crucial importance to the company and to each individual. In a series of programs conducted for down-the-line management, the Chairman and Chief Executive Officer, William Sneath, appeared at the outset in a short sound-movie segment explaining the importance of the program and using some of the same "buzz words" being introduced in the training seminar. It had a great effect on each participant group, adding significantly to the importance of the program.

Kennametal, a fast growing company in the high technology cutting tools business, uses a similar approach. With very few exceptions when he had to find a substitute, Quentin McKenna, Chairman of the company, appeared personally to start off each separate session. He explained why the program came into being and stressed its importance. It had a very positive effect on each class.

GAINING TOP MANAGEMENT SUPPORT

Given its importance, how can training directors get top management support? It is not an easy question to answer. Perhaps the question has to be rephrased to ask: what practical steps can training directors initiate and carry out that will, over time, strengthen top management support and thereby improve the organizational climate? Surely, training directors have some professional obligation to provide some leadership in affecting change. They should not sit idly by if they can see they are not getting the support they need.

Do Good Work

Doing good work is an essential starting point. Do the best possible job within whatever parameters or limitations have been set. No one can quarrel with this. During the long span of years that he headed up McKinsey & Company, one of the world's leading management consulting firms, Marvin Bower often said that by far the best way to market the firm's services was to do outstanding work for present clients. The same advice applies here. Make sure your training seminars are so good that people will talk about them. The only advice that might be added is to make sure your top management knows what a great job you are doing. But do so discreetly. Nobody responds well to a braggart.

Observe and Analyze

Another thought is to analyze your problem. Most successful sales representatives do a good deal of background research to assist in formulating a winning sales strategy with key prospects. Can you afford to do less in pursuing your own top target? Certainly not. Perhaps you can pick up some clues from his or her early upbringing. Is your chief old enough to have lived through the Great Depression? If so, you might expect some deeply ingrained values of thrift and conservatism. Was your chief raised on a farm as a hard-working member of a large family? Blue-blood or born of humble origin? It can make quite a difference. Study the text of letters to stockholders, speeches to security analysts, or other public utterances. Learn as much as you can from the chief's associates. Your observation and analysis should give you some clues as to appeals that might be successful.

One appeal that has proved successful in the past in gaining top-level support for management training is leaving a "monument" behind by way of a total professional management system before retiring. It is frequently frustrating to chief executives, a frustration that becomes greater as companies become larger, to realize what a limited impact they have on the day-to-day activities of the enterprise. One way for them to effect fundamental change is to launch a major effort to establish a more professional management culture or system in the enterprise, an effort that requires massive support from the training function to succeed.

Another appeal that can gain support for management training is to offer a means for the chief executive to instill a greater sense of common purpose or direction in an amalgam of semi-autonomous and separate businesses (divisions or subsidiaries). In the early 1970s, William S. Sneath, then President of Union Carbide Corporation, believed that the financial community viewed his corporate top management as a holding company or investment trust, providing limited leadership and coordination to an aggregate of many autonomous businesses. He wanted to establish an integrated, comprehensive management system to provide for more effective corporate direction while maintaining the benefits of decentralization. Implementation of the system involved a massive management training effort, from the very top executive team down through all levels of management throughout the world.

A further appeal incorporates the basic rationale for training: improving the productivity of human resources. Top management could be influenced to see training as the means for getting an edge on competition or coping with shrinking profit margins. This appeal would have a reach much broader than management training. It would include all forms of training.

Finally, the need to provide for orderly management succession might be another appeal. If a chief executive and other top executives are all within, say, five years of retirement, the time may be ripe for launching a management development and career planning program.

These appeals should be used carefully. You have to believe they are valid and can be effectively addressed through training. By all means, avoid creating unrealistic expectations as to what training can really accomplish.

Provide Proof

Providing proof, another means for winning top management, has two aspects: proving the need and proving the benefits. If you can develop specific, persuasive information on training needs and get them to the attention of management, you might well be successful in getting toplevel support. Some needs, like sales training or job instruction training, are not difficult to sell. The likelihood of success in getting other needs accepted will increase to the extent they are backed up by comprehensive, fact-founded needs analyses.

Proof by way of benefits or results should also be generated and merchandized. If the training program has been carried on for a period of time, you can make a special effort to follow up with past participants and their bosses to get specific evidence of productivity improvement or, at least, favorable quotes. If you are trying to start up a program, hard evidence is not easy to generate, but here are two ideas. Try to get success stories from other companies. Perhaps you have a professional colleague in another company who can help you get some persuasive information. A second way is to set up a "pilot program" with special emphasis on practical methods for identifying and capitalizing on operational improvements. Dedicated follow-up to a pilot program can often provide bottom-line benefits that are identifiable and measurable.

Overcome Objections

If you are having difficulty in gaining greater top management support, try to find out what the objections are and why they are coming up. You cannot deal with them unless you can pinpoint them clearly.

One of the typical problems you are likely to meet is budgetary: "We can't afford it." If the company is in fact doing well, this may be a "brush off." You have to probe more deeply to discover the real objection. If, on the other hand, it is sincere, your response might be, "We can't afford not to!" Then restate the benefits. Or, "We can prove to you that there will be measurable benefits that will exceed the cost." Then describe how. If you can anticipate the budgetary objection at the outset, then be sensitive to your timing. By all means, avoid the last two months before a new budget year, when budget cutting reigns supreme. Be patient. Wait until right after a good quarterly earnings report is released.

Another objection frequently encountered is this one: "We're too busy with other pressing projects." If this is a real objection, perhaps your timing was poor, in which case you gracefully retire and bide your time. If your company is always in a frenzy, always busy with a lot of projects, then your response could be, "All we want at this time is one 'pilot program' to prove its value to you; and we have chosen participants who are not involved in the other projects." Or, in the alternative, you might try this: "You are absolutely correct. That's why we are proposing that the first session should not start until next July. We can use the time between now and then to make doubly sure the program we have chosen meets our needs and is modified to conform to our terminology."

If you make a proposal and do get a negative response by the chief executive, do everything in your power to get a reason for the refusal. You have no way to cope with the problem unless you can identify the objection. Skilled sales representatives always probe for the buyer's real objection. In fact, they are happy to get it, because so often it results from a misunderstanding which can then be corrected, or from a lack of information which can then be supplied. The same could be true for you.

Proceed Step-by-Step

Another word of advice is to proceed step-by-step in lower levels of the organization to build a base of support. The step-by-step approach is the slowest and is something of a long shot. The top team may become so accustomed to thinking about the training function as something that exists for lower organizational levels that it will be more difficult to reach them in the future. The approach is the easiest one for the training director to follow. But if indeed it is the only feasible route to take, then care must be taken to accumulate success stories and to have these find their way upward to the chief and his staff.

Consider Consultants

Outside consultants can be of value, too, in this process of gaining top management commitment and support. Bringing consultants into the scene may in itself provide a rationale for a direct presentation to the top team. Usually consultants are highly skilled and quite persuasive in these top-level sessions. "A prophet is without honor in his own land," is an old and wise saying. Consultants can be valuable simply because they are *strangers*.

Top management might be responsive to the proposal that they become part of the process of selecting the outside consulting assistance. Point out that they need reassurance that the approach being taken by the consultants at lower levels is consistent with top management views. Then coach and counsel the consultants to get the maximum benefit from their presentation.

Don't Give Up

It is easy to get discouraged in this whole process. It often takes a considerable investment in time. It may involve emotional wear and tear through many disappointments and delays. But remember that circumstances can change. Changes in business conditions or changes of personnel in the executive suite can improve the likelihood of getting top-level support. In view of its powerful effect on the success of training seminars, especially management training seminars, it can be well worth the watchful waiting.

INFLUENCE OF PARTICIPANTS' SUPERIORS

A second powerful influence on the success of a seminar is that of immediate superiors of the seminar participants. The membership of this group is not constant. Presumably, it is the group that is being directly benefited through the training of its own immediate subordinates. These managers are the ones who send (or acquiesce in sending) participants to seminars in the first place; and they will receive the newly trained participants back on the job. It is in providing immediate supervision over these freshly trained subordinates back on the job that these managers can have a particularly important influence on how much of the new learning gets put to work.

Reinforcement

One way the influence of the participants' superiors can be felt is through reinforcement, or lack of reinforcement. It is a truism that an individual learns new skills mostly on the job under the coaching of the boss. Some training directors have said that skill building is 20% classroom and 80% on the job. Regardless of the precise percentage, the influence of participants' superiors on the job is crucial. If the boss played an active role in sending the subordinate to the seminar and in identifying specific improvement needs, you have a good chance for reinforcement on the job. The superior is very likely to discuss the seminar with the subordinate and provide on-the-job coaching to reinforce the improved behavior desired.

Unfortunately, the reverse can also be true. Participants' superiors can quickly undo the learning that took place in the seminar if they insist on or encourage behavior that is contrary to what was taught. For example: "I wouldn't waste my time writing up a mission statement with standards of performance. I know they teach you that in the course, but we all know what needs to be done here. Let's not waste time writing about it. Let's get down to work and do it." This kind of boss reaction will re-establish the behavior exhibited by the participant before the seminar. It will reinforce the individual's natural reluctance to change.

Modeling

The second influence comes through the modeling role of the immediate superior. Just as in the case of the chief executive, if the bosses of the participants consistently demonstrate the desired behavior, subordinates will more surely adopt it—and vice versa. The old adage that "action speaks louder than words" is particularly appropriate here. If, for example, a time management course offers a simple time planning form that participants see their managers using effectively, they are much more likely to use it themselves. If they have learned a five-step technique of delegation and see their superiors using the same method very effectively, they are most probably going to use it, too. Many managers, I believe, underrate the important modeling role that they play for their subordinates. Simply by setting a good example, managers can inspire subordinates to follow that example.

GETTING THE SUPPORT OF PARTICIPANTS' SUPERIORS

The importance of the participants' immediate superiors, particularly in the first three to six months after the seminar, is well recognized; but there is considerable frustration in doing something about it. Part of the problem stems from the time pressures on both the participants' superiors and on the training director. But part of it may be the lack of a clear, practical course to follow. For this reason it may be helpful to examine a number of approaches that are available. Getting the support of participants' superiors is difficult, but it can be done.

A Communication Campaign

One approach is to borrow ideas from professionals in advertising firms. These professionals have developed effective techniques for molding the attitudes of selected populations of consumers. They would undoubtedly tell you to clearly define your objective, develop attention-getting, high-impact messages to serve that objective and deliver them repeatedly through cost-effective media.

Why not try their approach to influencing the managers who will sooner or later be in this group of participants' superiors? The first thing you will discover is that the target population has to be more clearly defined. You will have to think separately about plant managers, sales managers, and data processing managers, for example. Suppose you take plant managers as your target population, just to illustrate the point.

Now, you have to clarify your behaviorial objective. What is it you want them to do? It may be to send people to seminars or to coach people who have returned from seminars to apply their new learning effectively on the job. These are different objectives that will require different approaches.

Let us say your behavioral objective is to get plant managers to send people to a course on supervisory management. You then have to ask yourself: what is the "unique selling proposition"? What key benefit will plant managers realize? Perhaps the answer is improved productivity of people. If so, this benefit becomes your communication objective.

Now, in developing copy to serve this objective you have to think of a "headline" right up front to capture attention. It should incorporate the key benefit in a high-impact way. Perhaps you could say: "Section heads at the Springfield Plant reported a 20% improvement in productivity after their supervisors attended the company's three-day supervisory training course." That message ought to interest the other plant managers. Possibly, you could use the message in transmitting the seminar schedule for next year, with a prominent red circle around the seminar to be promoted. After whatever elaboration is appropriate, your copy should end with your behavioral objective—a call to action. "Sign up for places in the seminar now, while there are still openings at the times of your choice."

The example used assumed a specific target population, a specific behavioral objective, and a specific program. The same approach could be used for other behavioral objectives and other target groups. By necessary implication, the least effective communication will be one promoting all seminars to all target groups.

One final thought before leaving the advertising analogy: why not develop a "tag line" to go with all your communications? It would not be part of each message, but a continuing reminder of the need for active line involvement both before and after the seminar. How about, "We need your help to help you best"? If you stop to think of it, you are in continuing, regular contact with the managers using your services. You are making needs analyses, announcing schedules of seminars, soliciting registrations, or confirming registrations. If you have organized a training committee, you are sending out reminders of meetings, agendas, background information for meetings, minutes, or progress reports. Think of the stream of written communications from your office. Suppose each one of these contained your own tag line in an attention-getting, high-impact way? Over time, it could have an effect.

Meeting Perceived Needs

Getting the participants' superiors involved in determining the training needs of their subordinates is another good approach. But make sure you meet those needs. If you can get these managers actively involved, they are more likely to use the services of the training function—and more likely to follow up in securing application on the job. A properly conducted needs analysis will get them involved. So will membership on a training committee. Sometimes informal discussions with individual managers will serve the purpose. But involvement in determining needs is not enough in itself. You have to meet those needs—and make sure the managers *know* you are meeting their needs.

Even though you want to get these managers actively involved in determining needs, there are times when you may have to shape their perceptions. After all, the training director is the professional in the field. You can't simply sit back and accept as gospel the perceptions of the group that constitutes participants' superiors. For one thing, they may have some misconceptions as to what training can accomplish. Some performance deficiencies or improvement needs may require other forms of corrective action, such as improvements in standards of performance, strengthening of feedback systems, or correction of motivational problems. You may have to "sell" these managers on some needs; and "unsell" them on others.

Partners in Selection

A third approach is to get participants' superiors to play an active role in scheduling seminars and selecting participants. As far as scheduling seminars is concerned, it is easier to get their involvement if special seminars are being set up to meet the needs of a specific group of managers—or easier yet, the needs of a single manager. The involvement comes directly out of the decision to go ahead. It is more difficult if a number of different courses are being "offered" to meet general categories of training needs. Typically, an annual program with many different courses has to be finalized six to eighteen months in advance of the actual seminar dates. But even in this case, you could circulate a "draft" or "coordination" copy of the proposed schedule for comments and suggestions.

The same difficulty exists in getting the participants' superiors to play an active role in filling up the seminars: they are too busy with other matters. If special seminars are being established to meet special needs, the superiors have already been involved and will quite naturally play an active role in selecting the participants. But for seminars scheduled to meet more general needs, participants' superiors and training director are frequently in adversary roles. The former tend to regard the immediate seminar as interfering with pressing operating needs. For this reason, they will favor postponing individual registrants to future seminars. Training directors, on the other hand, want to fill up their seminars. They find themselves in the position of pressuring managers to let their people go. In resolving this conflict, it is sometimes difficult to remember that the whole rationale for a training function is to provide a service to these line managers. If their role is perfunctory, they can hardly take an active interest in providing registrations or in post-seminar reinforcement. If they feel too pressured, they may not cooperate at all.

To some extent this conflict may be inevitable. But it can be lessened if the line manager can be induced to commit in advance a "block" of seats in a seminar series. Constant, continuing, two-way communication will also help.

Top-Down Training

Another way to win the support of participants' superiors is to cascade the seminar from higher to lower levels of management. In this way, superiors of any seminar group will have been through it first. If it is a good seminar, the superiors will more enthusiastically enroll their subordinates and more knowledgeably help out in the post-seminar application phase. The top-down approach is used effectively in management training, especially if the training is part of a larger program to make basic improvements in management practices, either through imposition of a mandated "management system" or desire to create a new management "culture."

Pilot Testing

Sometimes it is possible to get a higher level of management to "pilot test" a new seminar before their subordinates are put through the program. Essentially a variation of the top-down approach, it has an additional advantage: it solicits the participation of the higher level managers in the redesign or adaptation of the seminar. Even if the changes made are only in terminology, they provide an element of emotional ownership that adds greatly to the support provided by the seminar participants' managers.

Let me cite an appropriate example from our own experience. We use the term "Position Charter" in our management programs to describe a statement of the measurable results that a manager is accountable for achieving through the ongoing, continuing operations for which the manager is accountable. The Position Charter plays a central role in planning, organizing, appraising performance for purposes of individual development, and in establishing and exercising effective controls. The term was thought to be confusing in light of their existing management vocabulary by the top management group of Sea-Land Service, Inc., when they went through the program. Changing the term, at their initiative, to "Accountability Charter" made them view the whole program as more clearly their own.

Priming Participants

Getting participants' superiors to identify specific development needs for individual participants in advance of a seminar is another way to get their support. The approach is intended to motivate the participant to pay particular attention to his or her own training needs during the seminar. But it has the secondary benefit of stimulating the immediate superiors' interest in the seminar and encouraging the superiors to focus on the identified improvement areas after the seminar to assist in getting specific performance improvement.

Take as an illustration the subordinate whose interpersonal relationship skills are identified as a specific improvement need before a training seminar that includes this subject matter. Not only does the individual participant have a keener interest in the subject when it comes up in the seminar, but there is also a realization that the individual's manager will be looking for improvement on the job after the seminar. Then again, the manager, having had an involvement in creating this expectation, will feel a deeper sense of commitment to do the follow up.

PEER PRESSURES

The aggregate impact of peer group values, attitudes, and behavior is the third major environmental influence on the success of training seminars. Peer pressures make themselves felt before, during, and after the seminar. Potentially they can be fully as important as pressures from the participants' superiors, but are usually less intensive.

Attendance

For one thing, attendance at seminars can be affected by the overall opinions or attitudes of peers. If the feedback from past participants is favorable, the influence of the peer group is likely to be positive. Seminars are more likely to be well attended. Cancellations will be few. Seminar leaders know they start out with an advantage if individuals in a new group eagerly report on favorable experiences of specific past participants.

If, on the other hand, the influence is negative, training directors have to use every imaginable resource to fill up scheduled seminars. Cancelled seminars may involve cancellation charges and may be viewed as an admission of failure. Also, the few participants who specially arranged their schedules to attend the seminar are very likely to be upset at the change of plan.

Participant Commitment

The participants in every seminar are themselves part of this overall aggregation of peer values, attitudes and opinions. It is all brought with them into the seminar, although tempered by the particular mix of each participant group. The result can range from a very high level of commitment to a fairly low level; from an eagerness that is willing to take a great deal on faith, to a cynicism that will question and weigh everything.

Coming from one environment, a participant group might view the training seminar as a bit of well-earned rest and recreation. This is a concern that has been mentioned by training directors in large, country-club-like corporate education centers. This kind of a group will respond enthusiastically to the seminar leader's humorous stories. More often than not, they will intrude their own jokes into the discussion. One laugh invites another and everyone has a great time. But the learning experience will be weakened. Evening assignments will be given fast and superficial treatment. Distractions will easily be found.

It is easy for the seminar leader to fall in with a group like this, playing bridge or poker with them in the evenings, or a game of golf in the late afternoons. But there is a danger. The seminar leader may unwittingly encourage fun and games at the expense of real learning. One of our associates is an avid bridge player, but a very frustrated one because his wife dislikes the game. When he found a trio of good bridge players in his seminar group one time, he eagerly filled out a foursome and joined them at bridge on successive evenings during the seminar. His actions not only prevented his bridge companions from making a deep commitment to evening assignments, it set a bad example for the other participants.

In another situation, participants might arrive with a greater seriousness of purpose. They may have a keener realization of the benefits to be obtained in relation to on-the-job performance and ultimate advancement. Although such a group might still enjoy a good laugh, they will do a much more conscientious job of evening assignments and contribute much more to group discussions.

By way of illustrating the importance of participant attitudes, I had an uncomfortable experience early in my career as a presenter of management seminars. At that time, by way of an "ice-breaker," we used to ask participants to stand up, introduce themselves to the group, and tell about their expectations for the seminar. When I got around to the sixteenth participant, whom I shall call Norm Wilson, he stood up and said in a clearly hostile voice that he hadn't wanted to come to the seminar, that he was a lawyer, not a manager, and didn't see why he had ever been sent in the first place! Not only that, he refused to call me by my first name and was an irritant in group discussions from that moment on. The story turned out to have a happy ending, Norm Wilson making a complete turnaround—largely as a result of peer pressure. But the story illustrates the importance of participant attitudes, which can be shaped by the peer environment prevailing in the company and peer pressures in the seminar itself.

Post-Seminar Climate

Peer pressures that take place after the seminar represent a third way that peers can have an impact on the success of seminars. They contribute to the reinforcement, or lack of it, that the participant encounters back on the job. Just as immediate superiors are important in the post-seminar period, so too are peers.

Let us look first at some positive situations. Favorable reinforcement will occur if the subject matter of the seminar is in accord with methods that the participants' peers have found effective on the job and actually use themselves. It is even better if the participants' peers have been through the program, found it useful, and have incorporated the new behavior patterns into their work habits. Especially helpful is the situation that exists when authority figures within the peer group demonstrate an understanding of the subject matter of the seminar and its application in their work.

Each of these situations can easily be turned into a negative. If the participants' fellow workers do not follow the methods taught in the course, and make sarcastic remarks about the seminar, only the most self-reliant and committed participant will resist the pressure. The same is true when peers indicate that there is another established way that people want things done around here—forget the seminar. Even more damaging is to have authority figures in the peer group talk down the course or evidence behavior clearly inconsistent with the teachings of the course.

INFLUENCING THE PEER CLIMATE

In view of its importance, how can you influence the peer climate? Success in gaining top management and participants' superiors support will help in establishing a favorable peer climate, but will not be enough. There are additional approaches that training directors have to consider. One that has been recommended is to identify and measure the specific "norms" of the culture any particular training program is concerned with, and to use the knowledge gained in the design and administration of the program.* This idea might be particularly useful in gaining work group support during the post-seminar period. It could be applied with varying degrees of formalization, from questionnaires and structured interviews to informal discussions with the authority figures in a particular population. Probably the greatest influence training directors have on the peer group is the stream of people emerging from training seminars and returning to their places of work. The peer culture can be positively influenced by these past participants if a large proportion of the people in the various work groups have gone through the training and reacted favorably to it. But it is important that the behavior to be applied on the job is not inconsistent with group norms. The ideal situation is one in which participants are made to realize how they can personally benefit from applying the behavior change on the job.

In these ways you can influence the peer group; but the total organi-

* Allen, Robert F. and Silverzweig, Stanley: "Group Norms: Their Influence on Training Effectiveness," *Training and Development Handbook*, Chapter 17, McGraw-Hill Book Company, N.Y. 1976.

zational environment is created by the aggregate impact of peers, immediate superiors, and top management. Each of these groups has a major influence. None can be neglected. It is true that the ability of the training director to influence the environment will vary from organization to organization. It is also true that there are very real limits to how much can be accomplished. But, even if it takes time, it is worth the effort to try to make improvements. At the core of this effort is getting the greatest favorable impact from the programs that are being presented now. Then, over time, the scope and effectiveness of these programs can be increased through greater support from top management and immediate superiors and a more favorable peer climate.

Chapter 3

Organization and Staffing

Organizations can provide training seminars to their people without a formalized training function. A host of qualified outside firms and individuals are available to supply the service. Organizations of lesser size, perhaps five hundred employees or less, usually find it uneconomical to establish a separate training function. Typically, they combine the training responsibility into the total personnel or human relations function. However, for medium size to larger enterprises, say, one thousand employees and up, the training program will be much more effective if it is managed by an internal staff of qualified professionals, even if it is a very small one. In this chapter, you'll find some ideas and suggestions on how to organize and staff such a function.

RATIONALE FOR A TRAINING STAFF

By way of explanation, we have a fascinating case in our most popular management training program. It features Fred Nott, newly made president of a large conglomerate. Nott tries to make some fundamental changes in business direction and management concepts. But he faces an uphill battle. He has to win over a corps of managers who have been disciplined for 30 years to be loyal, unquestioning followers of the company's dynamic and autocratic founder. At the same time, in their own areas, these managers have been overbearing straw bosses. This deeply entrenched management climate is not an easy one for Fred Nott to change. After considering his challenge, our more alert participants conclude that in order for Fred Nott to succeed in making basic change in the management climate, he has to launch a broad-based management training program from top to bottom; and he has to back it up with qualified staff.

The reason for a specialized staff is to provide an ongoing focus of attention and a source of leadership, as well as a resource for providing advice and service (see figure 1). Line management's attention span on any subject tends to be rather short. There are constant interruptions from superiors, subordinates, customers, suppliers, regulators, labor leaders and community groups. Particularly in larger organizations, higher level executives have to depend on staff or consultants or both to do most of their in-depth thinking for them; and they have to depend

Figure 1

Scope of Advice and Service Provided by a Typical Training Department

RESEARCH	Training Needs Analysis Vendor Research Training Methods Research Program Follow-Up
PROGRAM DEVELOPMENT	Program Design Writing Testing Producing
PROGRAM DELIVERY	Discussion Leadership Individual Coaching Lecture
ADMINISTRATION	Program Procurement Program Scheduling Enrollment Securing Facilities Securing Equipment and Materials Participant Evaluations

on staff for sustained attention to any major, continuing concern or service need.

An Evolutionary Process

The need for organizing and staffing a training function tends to be evolutionary. It usually doesn't arise in quite as dramatic a way as it did for Fred Nott. In the early years of an enterprise, training and developing people occurs exclusively on the job. There is no formal training staff. As new people are hired, it is left to their immediate supervisors to train them in whatever skills they need on the job.

For some organizations, this situation continues even as they grow to substantial size. Some quite large professional service organizations, such as management consulting firms and law firms, do not formalize separate, discrete training functions. The same is true with a number of fairly large advertising, banking, and public utility companies.

Limitations of On-The-Job Training

Yet, most business enterprises of any size reach a point where it becomes economic to provide a specialized staff to help line managers carry out their responsibility for developing people. Especially where growth is rapid, or turnover high, the limitations of on-the-job training become apparent. The time demands on line managers to train their own people become too burdensome. Furthermore, the quality of instruction will vary widely from manager to manager.

Assume that in some hypothetical company one hundred managers spend an average of two hours a week training new people. That adds up to two hundred hours a week. If you can hire one training specialist to train these people in groups instead of singly, you might get the same number of people trained each week for a total outlay of only thirty-five teaching hours, representing the training specialist's time. In doing so, you free up two hundred hours of managerial time to do other, and perhaps more creative work. Perhaps you would need fewer managers, or could accommodate considerable further growth without establishing new manager positions.

The other major limitation of on-the-job training is that managers often are not very expert in teaching. By and large, line managers were put in their present positions for reasons other than their teaching ability. You can confidently expect this ability to be reflected in a normal bell-shaped distribution curve. Most of the managers will be fair to good; some will be excellent; and some will be very poor as teachers. Add to this thought the day-to-day operating pressures these managers face, and you have to push the whole curve toward the less able side of the graph. In your hypothetical company, it may take a great deal longer for new employees to become fully effective on the job if you rely on line managers alone to train them.

Advantages of a Permanent Staff

A well-functioning training department can offer many special advantages. It will supplement, not replace the line manager, whose on-the-job coaching will continue to play the major role in developing people. But a formalized training function will add to the effectiveness of that coaching in several ways.

Research. For one thing, the training staff has the time and ability to perform a research function. It can research the training needs of the company to establish a surer basis for determining the scope and nature of training that should be provided. It can keep in touch with the "state of the art," i.e., what other companies are doing. Its research activities can extend to determining the availability of off-the-shelf training programs and outside consulting services. The result could be to enhance greatly the cost-effectiveness of the training function.

Program Development. The training staff can also develop new programs or adapt existing programs more precisely and economically to meet the training needs that have been identified through research. The development or creative challenge presented can be most interesting and motivational for training staff people. They are undoubtedly in a better position than any outside resource to relate training programs more directly to the actual work environment. In practice, this program development role is most widely used for first-level supervisory training. At that level, where the largest supervisory population exists, the economies are most favorable.

Teaching. For most companies, the teaching role is the primary function of the department—to conduct training programs that result in desired on-the-job behavior change. It provides a great deal of flexibility for an organization to have its own corps of seminar leaders. Special programs can be scheduled on short notice; and ongoing training programs can be staffed much more economically from within as opposed to using outside consultants. The internal seminar leaders can learn from each other with a continuing upgrade in quality. Similarly, they will be strongly oriented to succeed, since their career progress so clearly depends upon doing a good job.

Evaluation. The training staff can also provide a means for constantly evaluating the effectiveness of ongoing programs, making improvements as necessary. This is done by the seminar leaders themselves, constantly experimenting with different ways to teach different subjects. Participant evaluations and audits offer further inputs. Whether training staff or outside seminar leaders are used, this evaluation function helps to ensure the quality of programs provided.

Consulting. Providing advice and service to top- and middle-level managers on all aspects of training needs and methods is a further benefit provided by a training staff. Generally accepted management theory makes line managers responsible for the training and development of their people, with the training staff available for advice and assistance. Much of this assistance is provided via the training department's ongoing programs. But from time to time, line managers need advice on whether or not training will help correct some performance deficiency, or how to establish development plans for individual employees, or perhaps how formal training can assist in some major operational change.

THE TRAINING MISSION

If you accept the need for a training function, the next step is to delineate clearly and completely what the training function is expected to accomplish. Until you clearly define its mission you cannot logically establish its organization structure or staffing needs. For example, you have to know that it is required to provide training in computer programming before you can plan a computer programming section and recruit people to staff it.

In offering suggestions on how to develop a satisfactory statement of the training mission, I will draw extensively from concepts which were originated by Louis Allen and have been incorporated in the management system espoused by Louis Allen Associates.* At the same time, recognizing the confusion over terminology that exists in the management community—especially planning terminology—I shall use terms for these concepts that I believe are most commonly used and most easily understood.

* See: Louis A. Allen, *Making Managerial Planning More Effective*, McGraw-Hill Book Company, New York, 1982.

The Mission Statement

Regardless of the words or term used, the first step in constituting a training function is to develop a statement of overall purpose or result to be achieved. I'll call it the "mission statement." The experience of many generations of successful managers leads to the conclusion that the mission statement should consist of four components that answer the questions why, what, who, and where.

Purpose. The first component of the mission statement describes the essential purpose or end result to be accomplished. It states *why* the training function exists. If it is functioning properly, the training department should be contributing significantly to the productivity of human resources in the enterprise. Other conditions and efforts also affect human productivity so that training cannot be held fully accountable for human productivity. But it can be held accountable for contributing to productivity. Furthermore, the training department should be contributing more value to the enterprise (even if that is difficult to measure) than it is costing. You can think of this difference as a *contribution* to the profit of the company, or to the basic purpose of the enterprise if it is non-profit. But you can be even more specific and say that the training function "contributes toward improved performance of human resources on the job and thereby contributes to the profitable growth of the company (or achievement of some other basic purpose)."

Product Line. The second of the four components of the mission statement answers the question: *what* is it of value that is being provided? The question relates not to the work that is being done, but rather to the end product or service being offered. One way of stating the product line component would be: "to provide a range of technical and management training programs and related services:" or to ask "What business am I in?"

Market. The product line component of the mission statement logically brings us to the next question: *who* uses or benefits from these programs and services? Who are the customers or clients? What is the market? For a training function, you could logically argue that there are two broad categories of people who benefit from the products and services offered: (1) line managers who draw upon the function to help them discharge their responsibility for developing their people, and (2) employees generally whose knowledge, attitudes, and skills are to be improved by participating in training programs.

Scope. The fourth component is especially important in large companies which may have both corporate and divisional training functions. The scope component describes *where* the product or service is being provided. It sets the limits within which the training department functions, for example: "The Corporate Head Office" or "The Household Appliances Division" or "Throughout the Company."

Putting this last component together with the three others produces a mission statement, which might resemble the following:

"The mission of the training department of (company) is to contribute toward the improved performance of human resources on the job and thereby contribute to the profitable growth of the company. The department will do so by providing a range of technical and management training programs and related services to meet the identified needs of managers and employees throughout the company."

Standards of Performance

The mission statement needs to be accompanied by measurable standards of performance. Otherwise it is too general. You can't really be sure you know what you are trying to accomplish. Nor can you know whether you are in fact accomplishing it.

Therefore, you have to define at the outset exactly what will constitute acceptable performance. Standards help everyone involved in or with the training function to visualize clearly what must be accomplished, to establish priorities, and to work more harmoniously with each other. Standards also provide a measurable basis for appraising performance and establishing controls as the training staff goes about its work. Those who work professionally with the management process know how difficult it is to develop measurable, realistic standards that will be acceptable and useful to the people whose performance is being measured. Yet, logically, the case for establishing and using standards is unassailable. Every training function ought to have them.

Key Factors. The starting point in developing standards for your mission statement is to think through the key factors or dimensions that will be sufficiently comprehensive but will nevertheless focus on the relatively few most significant aspects of performance that should be measured. Often these can be identified by thinking through "how much" will constitute acceptable performance; "how good" the results must be that are being generated; and "what cost" will be acceptable.

In the case of your training department, you might consider the key factors to be:

1. The *relevance* of the programs offered with respect to the identified development needs of individual employees and groups of employees,

2. The *quality* of those programs and services,

3. The *availability* of the department's services when needed, and

4. The *cost* of carrying on the training function.

Measurable Levels. The next step is to describe a measurable level of performance that it is necessary to achieve for each key factor. The statement does not necessarily have to be quantitative. For example, the existence of an annual plan approved by an Operating Committee could be a measurable standard. You either have such a plan or you do not have one. Therefore, it is measurable. In the case of your training department, you might consider the following as acceptable standards to use as a starting point in developing your own:

1. *Relevance.* The programs offered each year are responsive to a comprehensive needs analysis conducted at least every three years and reflect the priorities established by the Training Committee within the funds available.

2. *Quality.* 80% of the participants in each seminar evaluate the programs provided as 4.0 or better on standard evaluation forms; and 60% of participants' superiors in periodic follow-up surveys each year report identifiable improvements in participants' on-the-job performance.

3. *Availability.* In periodic, sample surveys at different management levels, three out of four respondents evaluate the training services reasonably available when needed.

4. *Cost.* The overall cost of training each year divided by the average total employee population does not exceed $__.

The foregoing standards are intended as "thought-starters" only. They have to be evaluated and modified to fit the needs of different training departments. A much more extensive statement was developed by the training department of Kraft, Inc. (see figure 2). But regardless of the exact format and terminology used, every training function should have an overall mission statement with standards of performance to articulate and delineate clearly the kind and quality of overall results to be achieved.

Figure 2
TRAINING & DEVELOPMENT DEPARTMENT MISSION

To contribute to the growth and profitability of Kraft, Inc., as specified by the management policy committee, by providing staff assistance in developing, maintaining, and improving on-job performance of managers.

Standards. This key objective will be accomplished successfully when the following standards are met:

1. *Needs Identification.* At least once each year, a written survey of specific corporate-wide management training and development needs is submitted through the sr. vice president of human resources to the management policy committee in order to establish priorities.

   This survey delineates:

   —The specific needs identified by key line and staff management
   —The level(s) of management involved for each specific need
   —The number of managers involved for each specific need
   —The potential resources available to address each specific need
   —A cost/benefit analysis for addressing each specific need
   —The number of seminars to be conducted for each specific need.

2. *Scope.* Within twelve months following establishment of priority needs, each need is addressed through a management training and/or development program designed to develop, maintain, and/or improve on-job performance.

3. *Program Development.* Each program is developed by either internal or external resources, meets pre-established specifications, and is completed on schedule and within budget.

4. *Program Delivery (Pilot and on-going).* Evaluations of the participants surveyed at the conclusion of the program indicate that:

   —90% evaluate the program as above average or better
   —90% rate the instructor(s) as above average or better
   —80% rate the meeting facilities and accommodations as satisfactory or better.

5. *Program Evaluation (Pilot and on-going)*
   A. At the conclusion of the program, 90% of the participants surveyed assess the subject matter as relevant to their needs.
   B. Within 90–200 days after each program, 80% of the participants surveyed and 80% of all the participants' supervisors surveyed cite specific on-job applications that indicate improved on-job performance by participants.

6. *Program Administration*
   A. Periodic survey of company-wide program needs and annual scheduling of programs to meet the given need.

Figure 2 (*Continued*)

B. Periodic survey of meeting facilities to determine which meet established program meeting criteria and are cost competitive.
C. Periodic determination of group leader needs for internally conducted programs, along with co-ordination of group leader selection, training, and evaluation, each based on established program criteria.
D. Maintenance of established program procedures, records, and materials.

7. *Services.* In periodic surveys of users, training and development services are rated as above average or better by 90% of respondents in terms of:

—Reasonably available when needed
—Oriented toward practical on-job applications
—Producing positive results
—Delivered efficiently
—Costs significantly less than the value provided.

STRUCTURE DESIGN

Once you have your mission statement, you can determine what work must be carried out to fulfill the mission and you can evaluate the various options you have for structuring that work. The product line component of your mission statement delineates the scope and kind of programs and services you have to provide. Similarly, the market and scope components will lead to some assumptions as to the total population to be served and hence as to the probable workload to be provided for in your organization.

Now, you have to consider the various options you have for structuring the work that must be done. To what extent do you want to get outside consultants or internal volunteers to do some of the necessary work? Should you have a single, central training function, or should you supplement a central staff with training capability nearer the point of service? Is it more effective to use a functional or a divisional form of structure in organizing a training staff?

These, and other organizational issues you will encounter can best be resolved by clearly identifying the acceptable options, developing sound criteria for evaluating the options, and selecting the option that best meets the criteria. By way of illustration, let me examine each of the three organizational questions mentioned above using the method proposed.

How Complete an Internal Capability?

The first question involves the extent to which you should establish complete internal training capability. You have a number of options. The first is to establish a complete internal capability, which seems to be the option adopted by a number of our industrial giants, such as General Motors, International Business Machines, and General Electric Company. A second option is to become mostly, but not completely self-reliant, as, for example, Western Electric Company. A third option is to use a balance of internal and external resources, as, for example FMC Corporation, Kraft Inc., and McGraw-Hill. And finally, a company can establish a training director position with no staff at all. In such cases, extensive use is made of outside consultants and internal, part-time volunteers.

Which of these options is best for any particular company? This is a question that can conveniently be resolved by developing evaluation criteria and evaluating the options against these criteria.

Training Workload. One criterion to be applied is the kind of training workload that is forecast. The assumptions you make as to workload will be important in determining how complete your internal capability should be. If you foresee your workload as sporadic, with occasional high peaks and possibly non-recurring, specialized demands, a minimum staff would be indicated. An ongoing, continuing base workload of some magnitude would favor staffing to that level, but not beyond. Otherwise, your training staff might generate training programs that are not truly needed in order to keep itself occupied.

Scope of Training. Another criterion would be the required scope of the training in terms of subject matter. The smaller the internal staff, the more likely it is that there will be limitations on what subjects it can teach at acceptable levels of quality. If internal trainers from other parts of the organization are to be used to extend the scope of training capability, much depends on your ability to train them. Outside consultants can also be used to extend the scope of your offerings, usually with high assurance of quality—if they are carefully selected.

Cost. No evaluation of your options would be complete without a consideration as to cost. The advantage on this criterion seems to go toward establishing an internal capability, assuming a reasonable level of continuing need. However, there are many hidden costs to be considered, such as fringe benefits, space, and service requirements. Using part-time, non-training department volunteers is also a relatively low-cost approach. Outside consultants cost more on a per-diem basis, but are still economic for handling peak loads, non-recurring needs or special requirements. For example, it is often less costly to use (or modify) an off-the-shelf program provided by outside vendors than it would be to develop a similar program from ground zero.

Centralize or Decentralize?

A second organizational question that arises in larger organizations is whether to have a central training function to serve all elements of the organization or establish training capabilities within each of the separate divisions of the company or, possibly, use a combination of the two. These are the options. A free choice among these options is usually not presented to a training director, since the larger companies are more than likely to have something in place already. Nevertheless, there are a number of criteria to evaluate in making or re-assessing this decision.

Organizational Policy. One of these criteria, perhaps the most important one, is existing organizational policy with respect to autonomous divisions. Some organizations are so highly decentralized that it would be inappropriate to have a centralized training function. Dover Corporation is a case in point. Other enterprises might already be highly centralized, such that a single training function serving all areas would be most easily accepted. Having a training capability at both corporate and divisional levels would be appropriate if consistent with organizational arrangements made for other staff services. Examples of the split arrangement would be R. J. Reynolds Industries and American Telephone and Telegraph Co.

Commonality of Training Needs. Another consideration is the existence of a significant volume of common training needs. Usually management training is a need common to all the operating divisions. But technical training needs may be quite diverse. For example, sales training is built around a body of universally applicable concepts and principles, but product line knowledge and specific selling skills may be so different from division to division as to preclude use of a single sales training program for the whole company.

Geographic Dispersion. A centralized training staff can function most effectively if its clientele is geographically convenient and of a single national culture. Large multi-national corporations have had some success "exporting" seminars to other countries. But because the central staff's impact is necessarily limited, local training capabilities are virtually essential. The geographic factor is less significant within the U.S.A., but combined with other reasons can contribute toward at least some decentralization.

Other Considerations. In any particular instance there may well be other evaluation criteria. Some divisions may represent recent acquisitions with well-established training functions, which might most easily be continued at the division level. In some organizations there may be a special value placed on cross-fertilization of ideas or improving communications generally across divisional lines. If so, a central training function will provide opportunities for employees from different divisions to associate with each other in a seminar setting. Cost should also be mentioned, although there are trade-offs. Direct salary costs for the total training function will probably be less if centralized. But the cost of participant travel and maintenance could off-set this cost saving if participants have to travel significantly greater distances to attend centrally sponsored seminars.

Functional or Divisional?

If the company or enterprise as a whole is organized divisionally, a further organizational question may be presented: whether to organize training along functional or divisional lines, or some practical combination of the two. The question may be presented at the corporate or divisional training department or both. Figure 3 provides organizational charts illustrating each option. Again, the question is more likely to be raised if the training group is of sufficient size to provide options.

Cost. Cost is almost always one basis for reaching a decision on this question. Frequently, but not necessarily, the purely functional organization will be more economic, either in terms of outright cost or cost related to productivity.

Specialization. The advantages of specialization also have to be considered. A functional organization will usually offer more opportunities for skill specialization. The type of skills necessary for excellent work in program development are different from those required for the most effective delivery of training programs. A person specializing in program development will bring a higher level of expertise to bear than would two people each spending half of their time on program development. And similarly for program delivery, one who specializes in seminar presentation develops greater skill than another who does it part-time only.

Accountability. On the other hand, the divisional structure should provide a more complete accountability for results. If the individual who develops a program also has to present it, there is only one person to claim the success or bear the brunt of failure. In a functional structure, the one who presents the program can blame the program developer if something goes wrong, and the program developer can blame the presenter.

User Liaison. Divisionalization by user group or a mixed form with user group liaison positions (see Figure 3) would have to be favored,

Figure 3

FUNCTIONAL VERSUS DIVISIONAL ORGANIZATION OPTIONS

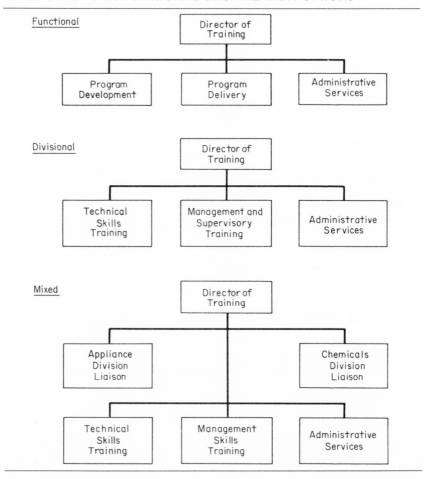

if different user groups have clearly distinctive training needs, or strongly believe this to be the case. Each user group has a clearly defined point of contact with someone in the training function who spends full-time responding to or advancing the interests of that group. The mixed form, with its liaison positions, is more appropriate for large organizations where the additional cost of those positions may well be worth the faster response to user needs.

STAFFING CONSIDERATIONS

Once you have established the organization structure, the next logical steps are to (1) define each position provided, (2) set a salary grade for each position, (3) determine the qualifications required in the individual to be selected for each position, and (4) find the right person for the job.

Defining The Positions

The mission statement that was created in order to define the purpose of the total training function can now be used as a definition of the position occupied by the head of the department, the training director. The other positions established in the training function can be defined in the same way. In the alternative, a position description can be developed for each. But regardless of format or descriptive title, we believe these points should be covered in a written definition of each position:

1. The objective or overall results to be accomplished by the position, including a summary statement of the products or services provided, the clientele or customers served, and the dimensions or scope of the position.
2. Measurable standards that will be used to determine when that overall result is being successfully achieved.
3. Management or supervisory duties.
4. Primary technical duties and responsibilities. These need not be all inclusive and should not be too verbose.
5. Significant working relationships with other elements of the organization.

Figure 4 contains an actual example of a position description for the training director of a medium-sized company that meets most of these five points.

Figure 4

POSITION DESCRIPTION*

SUMMARY OF POSITION:

This position is responsible for planning, administering, and coordinating corporate manpower planning, management development, and employee educational and training programs; providing guidance to area management in assessing the management potential of their employees and in determining the scope of training and development needed to prepare these employees for future management positions, and directing the administration of employee educational, skills development, and career counseling programs.

DIMENSIONS:

Total Corporate Staff:
Operating Budget:
Salary Budget:
Tuition Refund Program Reimbursements:

NATURE AND SCOPE:

This position reports to the assistant vice president, organization development as do the corporate staff psychologist, the manager, employment, and the coordinator, equal employment opportunity. Reporting to the incumbent are the coordinator, management development, the coordinator, corporate training, the training aide, the meeting scheduler, and a secretary.

The corporate training and manpower planning and development area is responsible for the development and implementation of corporate manpower planning, management development, and employee educational and training programs in order to ensure competent manpower to meet corporate operational and service needs.

The functions of this position include:

Supervision:

The incumbent plans, organizes, and directs the work of the supporting staff and is responsible for recommending and implementing policy and procedure changes to meet corporate training and development needs.

This includes responsibility for the placement, training, and promotional movement of employees, approving salary increases, and ensuring personnel actions to further the morale of the employees. In addition, the incumbent delegates assignments and provides guidance and expertise on appropriate training and development procedures to be utilized in resolving the more complex and/or sensitive problems which are beyond the scope of the supporting professional staff. This also requires providing supervision to a clerical staff responsible for scheduling meeting room reservations, maintaining train-

* Manager Corporate Training & Development, Blue Cross/Blue Shield of Greater New York, used here with permission.

Figure 4 (*Continued*)

ing facilities and equipment, assisting in the preparation of training and development materials, and performing related clerical and typing duties.

Human Resource Planning Program

The manager is responsible for coordinating and administering the human resource planning program which evaluates and assesses the potential of management employees for promotion to the next management level and determines common and specific training needs which must be met in order to prepare these employees for future management positions. This involves meeting with assessors to provide them with the necessary training to conduct assessment feedback interviews and to complete the assessment forms properly. In sensitive management evaluations, the incumbent will assist management in reaching agreement about an employee's potential where conflicting management opinions exist. As a result, the individual will plan and coordinate the appropriate training needed including formal classes, job rotation, and referral to outside consultants or attendance at local schools.

Manpower Planning and Development

The incumbent is responsible for providing guidance and direction in analyzing the corporation's immediate and future management manpower needs. In addition, the individual receives and analyzes a forecast of general labor market conditions and its impact on the corporation's labor needs. The individual formulates and implements training and development policies and procedures to facilitate the existence of qualified management for future management positions. This requires providing management with the necessary information required to develop long-range plans for the selection, recruitment, and training of employees by providing the necessary training and development for current management or determining the need to recruit qualified management from the outside labor market.

Management/Corporate Training Programs

The incumbent is responsible for developing an annual schedule of management development and skills training classes based on a complete analyses of training program requests and common training needs in the corporation. The individual will design or supervise the design of training program content, methodology, and evaluation techniques to meet these training needs. In addition, the incumbent must evaluate and determine the most appropriate training methods and techniques to be utilized in meeting corporate training needs. The incumbent must coordinate and monitor all formal classes in order to ensure that training programs are responsive to training and development needs. Training programs are evaluated by obtaining trainee feedback and suggestions for improvement and conducting interviews with immediate supervisors to determine whether the trainee's behavior has changed.

Figure 4 (*Continued*)

Career Counseling

The incumbent is responsible for providing educational counseling to all levels of management, up to and including vice president level. The educational counseling could include information on the tuition refund program, degree programs, courses, and outside consultants. The individual will also assist management to set career goals and to show them how their career goals can be achieved. The employee maintains liaison with employment concerning current and future job openings and is familiar with the functions and skills needed for various jobs in the company in order to counsel employees properly. Consideration must also be given to EEO implications, employee goals, advancement, and future use of skills in providing guidance to employees on advancement opportunities.

Special Assignments

As assigned by the assistant vice president, organization development or on own initiative, the incumbent will prepare or supervise the preparation of special reports and projects. The individual must analyze and determine the priority of corporate training needs and conduct a complete cost analysis in order to determine the benefits achieved and the extent of a training program's impact on corporate operations. To ensure appropriate actions by concerned parties, the incumbent monitors all activities and provides the necessary guidance relative to the management training program, the tuition refund program, the Colman scholarship program, the Adelphi internship program, and the CETA program.

The incumbent develops, as part of the human resource planning program, the appropriate procedures for implementing job rotation to provide employees with broader experience in preparation for future management positions. Studies are also conducted to analyze the effectiveness of the tuition refund program and the secretarial training program in meeting corporate goals. Special projects to be accomplished include working with EEO coordinator in the development of an EEO training program for management personnel to keep them abreast of the various anti-discrimination laws and the necessary procedures to be implemented within their areas to ensure EEO compliance.

As a member of a committee to design a new performance appraisal system, the individual provides recommendations for inclusion of job and personal career goals within the parameters of the new system. The incumbent is also responsible for preparing a catalogue on training and development programs and services which will provide descriptions on management programs offered by the department.

As a major assignment, the incumbent will be developing a new management training program which will provide a well structured corporate orientation for management trainees in order to inform them of major corporate

Figure 4 (*Continued*)

operations. An important consideration is the identification of qualified coaches in management who will provide the necessary guidance and support to the management trainees during their rotation through different workflow operations. Also the individual must monitor closely all phases of the program and evaluate the effectiveness and accomplishments achieved by the program.

This position has internal contact with all levels of management and training personnel throughout the company. External contacts include management development and training personnel from other companies and plans, management consultants, college admission officers, and instructional material and equipment vendors.

This position requires advanced education in education principles, training methods and techniques, and industrial relations; extensive experience in training and management development, human resources systems, skills inventory, and career counseling. Excellent communication skills, administrative and management abilities are also required.

SPECIFIC ACCOUNTABILITIES:

1. Plans, organizes, and directs the work of the supporting staff and is responsible for implementing policy and procedure changes to meet corporate training and development needs.

2. Provides the necessary guidance and expertise on appropriate training and development procedures to be utilized in resolving the more complex and/or sensitive problems which are beyond the scope of the supporting professional staff.

3. Coordinates and administers the human resource planning program which evaluates and assesses the potential of management employees for promotion and determines common and specific training and development needs which must be accomplished in order to prepare employees for future management positions.

4. Provides management with the necessary information to develop long-range manpower planning goals.

5. Supervises or designs a variety of training programs including program content, methodology, and evaluation techniques to meet corporate training needs.

6. Provides specific career counseling to management employees in order to assist them in determining the most effective means of achieving their educational and development goals.

7. Prepares or supervises the preparation of special reports and projects in order to implement or revise training and development activities within the corporation.

In defining the position, it is well to consider the possibility of establishing "pass-through" positions, positions that are established for people to occupy for one or two years and then move on. Establishing pass-through positions can bring a continuing influx of new ideas, experience, and enthusiasm, and offset the risk of stagnation. The Western Electric Company uses this approach to supplement a highly qualified "core" training staff in its Corporate Education Center in Hopewell, New Jersey. The approach is sometimes used with special effectiveness in sales training. Sales trainers have more credibility if they speak from successful personal experience. The Western Union Telegraph Company has used this approach. So has Xerox Corporation.

Establishing the Salary Grade

In setting a salary grade for the position, you have to be guided by the latest compensation surveys. Our own observations suggest a fairly direct relationship between pay level and effectiveness. If a company is serious about wanting to improve the productivity of its human resources, it ought to pay enough to get the talent needed to do a better than average job. The American Society for Training and Development conducts salary surveys periodically that can serve as a useful point of reference in setting salary grades.

Establishing the Qualifications

Setting position qualifications, the proven skills and experience required to perform the job successfully, depends necessarily on the position to be filled. Nevertheless, here are some ideas of general applicability:

1. Experience: At least three to five years experience in training, including program development as well as presentation, except for entry-level jobs.
2. Record of Success: A record as an achiever—getting things done, and done well; and getting things done through others.
3. Communicating Skills: Considerably above average in both oral and written communications.
4. Intelligence: A quick and logical mind, with a better-than-average academic record.
5. Personality: A likeable person, interested in and sensitive to other people, with a good sense of humor, a high energy level and considerable self confidence.
6. Potential: Someone with the potential for advancement.

This last qualification suggested may not be wholly self-explanatory. You should guard against an individual's staying in the position so long as to "go stale." Fresh blood every five to ten years can keep the function a vital one. Much can be said for using the position as a training ground for higher positions in the human resources field, or as a means for rotation of people within that department.

Filling the Position

As in filling any position, you have to remember these well established guidelines in staffing the training function:

1. Consider inside as well as outside candidates.
2. Get a large number of candidates, if possible.
3. Make a rough preliminary screening against the qualifications.
4. Hold a first interview.
5. Notify candidates no longer to be considered.
6. Make telephone checks with previous supervisors and past seminar participants.
7. Verify educational achievements and previous employment.
8. Audit platform skills, if practicable.
9. Hold final interview, multiple interviews if possible.
10. Make decision.
11. Notify all candidates.
12. Develop plan for successful introduction of candidate.

Selecting your people, the last step in the process of organizing and staffing the training function, is of special importance. The success of the training seminars you put on will depend very heavily on the ability of the people you choose to develop the programs, conduct them, and provide back-up support. There are few, if any, "back room" people in training. They are all out there working with others in the company, representing the function almost every day. They will function more effectively in a soundly organized department. As a result, the training seminars you sponsor are far more likely to be effective in improving the performance and productivity of the human resources in your company.

Chapter 4

Using Outside Resources

Training directors almost invariably supplement their internal capabilities through the selective use of outside educational institutions and consultants, for some very practical reasons. Decisions on when to use outside resources, to whom to turn, and how to work most productively with them can have a major influence in getting the most out of your training seminar dollars.

THE PROS AND CONS

In any specific situation, the first question is whether to use outside resources at all. The reader may feel that I am somewhat prejudiced in dealing with this subject, with some twenty-four years of consulting experience behind me. But in self-defence, let me point out that I was in the "outside world" for five years and made considerable use of consultants from the client side of the fence. Perhaps more importantly, I have learned over the years that there has to be a good fit between what the client needs and what the consultant has to offer. In order for a consulting relationship to be truly productive, both the client and the consultant must benefit from it.

The Potential Benefits

The reasons why so many training directors turn to outside resources are numerous. Some will be more important and others less so, depending upon the extent to which the training function has been deliberately established to be self-sufficient and the kind of assistance needed.

Extension of Capabilities. A most frequent reason given for using outside resources is to broaden the "product line" of the training department. In some cases, there may be no inside trainer with the knowledge and experience needed to conduct the seminar. Then again, there may be sporadic needs for specific expertise that can be most conveniently met through some outside resource. In other cases, training directors may want to offer more courses than could be provided if only internal trainers were used.

Time-Saving. Another potential benefit is to save program development time. If there is a clear training need and no existing program in-house to meet the need, an outside resource may be the best answer. The saving is not only in the commitment of the training department's human resources, which could be considerable. It is also in the possibility of an earlier start-up of the program, which could be important in certain cases.

There is a potential danger here. About four years ago one of the major commercial banks in New York City purchased an off-the-shelf, modular program on professional management. It wasn't quite what the training director wanted, but she thought that her staff could do some substitution and supplementation that would make it ideal for her purposes. What she didn't anticipate was the creative momentum that the project developed in her staff. They kept finding so many ways to make the program better that the original vendor's program was hardly discernible in the end product. Instead of trying to save time and money, she later admitted, she would have been better off starting from scratch.

Program Quality. In choosing between internal program development and use of outside resources, training directors often conclude that there is greater assurance of program quality if they can find a vendor with the right program. This assurance increases with the number and quality of successes the vendor can claim. Furthermore, there are other clients using the program who can testify to its quality. Sometimes it is possible to audit the program. For all these reasons, there can usually be a good assurance of program quality.

Credibility. An outside consultant can offer greater credibility, particularly for higher level groups in an organization. Inside trainers are often of equal or lesser rank and stature than the participants, which can have a negative influence on credibility. A visiting consultant can often bring impressive credentials and wide experience from a large number of different companies that help create high credibility.

Easy Discontinuance. Arrangements made with outside consultants are generally terminable at any time, with the exception of certain government contracts. On the other hand, the development of a full-time internal staff brings with it a commitment to keep them gainfully employed. If for any reason, such as budgetary cut-backs, the training workload is reduced, serious personnel problems can be presented.

More Dispassionate Evaluation. As a final, and more arguable point, training departments may be more objective in evaluating the impact of programs brought in from the outside. They still have an involvement, since they perceived the need and brought in the outsiders. But there is not the same emotional involvement that is likely to exist in programs they developed themselves. Failures attributable to the outside consultants are easier to bear than their own. Even if the training department is in fact objective, they would appear to be biased in evaluating the worth of their own programs, which could effect the credibility of their conclusions.

Possible Disadvantages

Notwithstanding all these potential benefits, there are also some possible negatives. As in any decision-making process, both the advantages and disadvantages have to be weighed in order to arrive at a logical conclusion.

Loss of Control. The first of these disadvantages is that the training director no longer has direct, hands-on control of the seminar. Even if nothing goes wrong, there is always the potential. Educational materials may not be received on time, or the wrong ones may be delivered. Scheduling problems may prevent getting the right person from the consulting firm to conduct the seminar. Or a last minute substitute may be presented. Sometimes the outsider, for lack of full understanding of the company and its practices, may make statements in answering questions or in group discussions that may have an unfavorable effect on other programs offered by the training department or on company practices. The more completely an outsider understands the company, the less likely this is to happen.

Risk on Relevance. Use of a standard program from an outside resource represents to some degree a compromise from the ideal, although the risk can often be minimized. In management seminars, the consultant's standard educational materials are likely to use a different terminology in the area of planning. Perhaps there are minor differences with other seminars being offered by the company as, for example, on decision-making or motivating. Inconsistencies such as these can detract from the cumulative impact of the training program.

The risk can be minimized by making a thorough review of the educational materials before retaining the consultant. Then, if appropriate, substitutions or additions can be made to these materials. Or, in the alternative, the presenter can be required to adjust his presentation to avoid confusion, as by making cross references to the other courses.

Expense. A further consideration is expense. Consulting firms have to price their programs and services to recoup sometimes surprisingly high program development costs. They also have to pay well to attract and keep the professional talent they need—especially in light of heavy away-from-home travel schedules. As a result, per diem rates well into four figures are common, although individual practitioners may charge considerably less. Somewhat less costly on a per-participant basis are vendors' off-the-shelf programs conducted by vendor-trained in-house trainers. The cost advantage per participant increases as the trainee population passes and exceeds roughly thirty to forty people in number.

OUTSIDE RESOURCES AVAILABLE

If, for a particular training need, a training director finds the advantages outweigh the disadvantages, the next question is what outside resources are available to meet that need.

Sources of Assistance

Broadly speaking, there are two kinds of outside resources available: institutions and consultants. The precise line between these two is somewhat blurred. But the non-profit educational institutions, such as Harvard Business School and Stanford Business School, are quite different from professional training and development firms in basic orientation, type of programs and services offered, and fee schedules.

Institutions. On the institutional side, there are established educational institutions offering courses in various subjects that training directors can use to meet specific individual needs. Not all of these offerings come under the heading of "seminars," but most of them do. Special industry programs also have to be included on the institutional side. The College of Insurance, for example, supported by the insurance industry, provides a wide variety of seminars needed by insurance company training directors. The National Association of Savings Banks, for another example, has sponsored an extensive training program for its membership.

Vendors of equipment could be considered another type of institution. They typically provide training in the use of their equipment. The telephone companies have long been leaders in the field. Training is also available as part of the selling package in selling other equipment, such as word processors.

Consultants. The other, and perhaps primary outside resource, consultants, range in type from individual practitioners to large, multinational firms. The individual practitioner, frequently a college professor providing consulting services on the side, can offer a great deal of flexibility in meeting training director needs—and usually at a much lower cost than the established consulting firms. It is difficult to generalize about the individual practitioner since everything depends on the individual. There are so many individual consultants in the market that it is extremely difficult to find just the right one. Training directors are besieged by literature and telephone calls from these people. So much so that their secretaries become skilled in explaining to telephone callers that their bosses are "in conference" or "away from their desks." This gives the training director the option to call back or not—usually not! If you're lucky enough to find a really good individual consultant, take good care to keep and nurture this valuable resource.

The established professional firm will typically offer a broader range of services and provide greater assurance of quality, both in programs and in personnel. In using such a firm you are not completely dependent on a single individual; you have access to the pooled experience and skills of the whole firm. On the other hand, they tend to be considerably more costly than the individual consultant.

Scope of Services Provided

By far the greatest use made of outside consultants is in providing off-the-shelf programs and in seminar presentation. Yet outside resources are available for a wide range of services. Each type of assistance available may be useful depending on the particular situation.

Needs Analysis. Outside consultants can assist in making a needs analysis. Several firms offer a questionnaire/follow-up interview program designed to identify and prioritize management development needs in any given manager population. Other firms provide means for pin-pointing special individual needs in advance of scheduled attendance at management seminars. But in most cases, training directors prefer to make their own needs analyses. They find that they can do it more cheaply and quickly and it gives them the opportunity to interface meaningfully with users of their services.

Program Development. Another service provided is developing training programs to meet specific needs. Contracting for program development tends to be expensive if tight specifications are established. With a little leeway, consultants can sometimes piece together parts of established programs which can reduce the cost. Sometimes it is possible to negotiate a cost-sharing arrangement in which the program is developed deliberately to be generic and becomes the property of the consultant to sell to other clients. In these arrangements it may be possible for the client to recoup its out-of-pocket development costs through a percentage reduction in the standard fees charged by the vendor for the continuing use of the program.

Program Adaptation. The line between program development and program adaptation is not too clear-cut. But one important service outside firms can provide is to "package" their standard educational materials in workbooks that carry the client's logo. For additional expense, changes can be made in terminology, emphasis, or sequence. The end result is customizing the program to look like the client's own, while at the same time providing the quality assurance of a proven, standard program.

Presentation. One of the most commonly used services consultants provide is to come in and to conduct their own standard programs or programs they have developed or customized. Budgets permitting, this is probably the quickest and easiest way for training directors to extend the scope of their offerings. Not a great deal of lead time is required. Nor is the administrative burden too demanding.

Off-The-Shelf Programs. Reportedly the largest revenue producer to vendors in the training business is the sale of standard, off-the-shelf programs conducted by in-house trainers given special training by the vendor. Use of these programs saves program development time, offers good assurance of quality and is quite cost-effective for large populations. Arrangements for purchasing these programs differ with different vendors. In some cases there is a one-time charge for the program and a fee payable for each participant going through the program, for which needed educational materials are supplied. In others, there is only the continuing fee or royalty as participants go through the program.

Training the in-house trainers may be included in the one-time price or may entail additional professional fees. Some vendors will insist on their own certification of trainers in order to give them a continuing control over quality. They view this as a protection for the client as well as themselves.

Auditing. Consultants are also available to audit and coach in-house presenters. In most cases, this service has to be agreed to at the outset and be part of any overall contract for off-the-shelf programs. If it is not, there are natural inhibitions. Consultants want their time to be specifically billable; they don't want to give their time away. The in-house trainers, on the other hand, probably prefer not to be audited.

Individual Consultation. A further service sometimes provided is assistance in making needs analyses for individual participants before the training seminar, which is combined with post seminar follow-up. The service is performed via questionnaires given to superiors, subordinates, and peers as well as to the participant. The questionnaires are followed up by personal interviews and some personal coaching at the seminar. If this approach is acceptable to the client people involved, it can be very productive.

Follow-Up Evaluation. On occasion, consultants are used to assist in the evaluation of results achieved in training seminars. When used, the service is typically part of a larger program in which in-house trainers have been conducting the consultant's program. In these cases, the evaluation is directed more towards the effective use of the program rather than the program itself. But the service can be extended to include surveys of past participants or their managers. This type of service is not often used, possibly because the consultant is not in an independent, objective position. There would almost necessarily be a bias in favor of reporting positive results from using the consultant's own programs.

SELECTING THE OUTSIDE RESOURCE

At one time or another, most training directors will face the need to select an outside resource. They will have to determine what outside resources to consider and how to go about selecting the one that will prove to be most effective. Here are some suggestions that might serve as a starting point in developing your own selection criteria.

Calibre of People

First and foremost has to be the overall effectiveness of the specific individuals who would be providing the service. If an educational institution is involved, a good source for checking on the calibre of the individuals providing the service is people who have gone through the program in the past. In the case of consultants, a personal audit is the best reassurance of quality and is often easily arranged. Telephone or face-to-face checks with present or former clients are also important, although the consultant is likely to supply only favorable references.

Many training directors maintain a network of professional relationships that can be helpful in checking out both institutions and consultants. Personal acquaintances are more likely to be objective. But make sure their opinions are based on personal experience rather than hearsay.

The calibre of people providing the service is more important for consultant-led programs than it is for off-the-shelf programs conducted by in-house trainers. There is a greater, continuing exposure directly to user groups. Nevertheless, the quality of the training offered to your in-house trainers does depend on the quality of those in the consultant's organization who will do the training.

Quality of Educational Materials

The quality of the educational materials to be used is critically important, both for consultant-led and client-led seminars. Although it is very time consuming, training directors are well advised to review these educational materials carefully and thoroughly; not just the participant workbooks, but the audio-visual accompaniments as well.

One example of the importance of inspecting the visuals is provided by one leading vendor of off-the-shelf programs. Professional actors were used with considerable success in one program to produce 35mm visuals accompaning narrated audio tape portions. But it was an expensive way to go. Then a few prospective clients reacted negatively. They believed the characters didn't really look like the people you see in offices every day. Accordingly, the firm involved decided, in producing a specialized industry version of the same program, to use actual employees of the company for whom the specialized version was being made. While in a sense more realistic, the result was not visually pleasing to many people. Perhaps people are all so brainwashed by television and commercially produced movies these days that we always expect to see beautiful people. At any rate, the new, specialized version of the program was criticized because the characters were too ordinary and unattractive.

Another problem with visuals is the unexpected way they can become "dated." When the original version of the program mentioned above first came out, it was at the height of the mini-skirt fashion. It was also the "in" thing at that time for women to wear bouffant hair-do's. Within only a few years, the skirt length looked positively indecent and the hair style completely inappropriate in a business setting.

Adaptability

A third selection criterion, adaptability, applies particularly to consultants rather than institutions. Those who have been involved in sales training know the importance of satisfying the customer's need rather than selling a product. This concept can be applied as well to selecting consultants. A consultant's greater willingness to adapt materials to your needs can make that consultant clearly more valuable than another. In many cases, the cost of adapting standard programs may preclude any adaptation; nevertheless, a readiness on the part of the consultant to discuss adaptations imaginatively can be a real plus. Often it is possible to find approaches that make the outsider's programs more relevant without prohibitive increases in cost.

Scope and Depth of Available Resources

The depth and breadth of resources available is one clear advantage that an established firm has over the individual consultant. The client is not limited by the knowledge and skills inventory of a single person, nor dependent on the continuing health and availability of that person. Established firms typically ensure that at least a second member of the professional staff is known to the client and available for back-up if necessary. This second person also gives the primary consultant a resource to turn to for advice or simply to get a sounding board for ideas. Then again, if the training director comes up with a new need, the established firm is more likely to be able to meet that need than is the individual practitioner. Once a training director has established a mutually satisfactory relationship with an outside firm, it saves a lot of trouble to turn to the same firm for other programs. The firm starts off with a good knowledge of the company and its people. Also, you can be sure that the additional program will be completely consistent with the first both in concepts and vocabulary.

Cost

An ever-present consideration is cost. Training directors have to operate within established budgetary constraints. They have to commit their available resources wisely to get the greatest return for their money. In a very rough approximation, as the first four selection criteria are given greater importance, the cost of using outside resources tends to increase. The selection decision, therefore, turns very frequently on getting an optimum balance between cost, on the one hand, and on the other: calibre of individual consultants, quality of program materials, adaptability, and extent of available resources.

GUIDELINES IN NEGOTIATION

If you have proceeded to the point where you have decided to use an outside resource and have made a selection against the criteria suggested, the next step in the process is to negotiate the arrangements. See Figure 5 for a suggested checklist of items. Some of them are worth special elaboration.

Figure 5

NEGOTIATING CHECKLIST

1. Clear and specific delineation of program or service to be provided
2. Program cost
3. Professional fees entailed
4. Expenses to be reimbursed
5. Other costs entailed (the facility, audio-visual equipment, shipping charges, etc.)
6. Commitment on named individual consultants to provide service
7. Participant evaluations
8. Participant completion certificates
9. Trainer certificates
10. Action steps to be taken
11. Schedule
12. Replacement of lost or damaged audio-visuals and Leaders' Guides
13. Cost of future educational materials
14. Training future trainers
15. Rights to use copyrighted materials
16. Termination

Copyrights

Make sure what rights you have to reproduce and use copyrighted educational materials. You may want to be able to incorporate extracts or ideas from these materials into company manuals. Most vendors will allow this if you give appropriate credit on cover pages. They will be much freer in allowing it if the subject is brought up during the initial negotiations. On the other hand, you have to realize that these educational materials have in most cases been developed at great expense. They represent the "bread-and-butter" of the vendor's business. It would be improper to reproduce and re-use these materials yourself or to copy materials to avoid further obligation to the vendor.

A case in point is provided from our own practice. By accident, we happened to hear from an employee of one of our clients that one of our off-the-shelf programs was being conducted very successfully in the company. Checking our own records, however, we found that we had received no orders for participant workbooks, which meant that they were reproducing copyrighted workbooks we had sold to them at an earlier time. We were able to get hold of one of these photocopied workbooks and confronted the president of the company with the evidence. He was properly upset and ordered full payment to us for all the workbooks they had made and used for themselves. He made it abundantly and uncomfortably clear to the training director involved that such actions were not in keeping with the ethical standards established by the company.

Termination

Another point to remember is the need to include a fair and convenient way to provide for cancelling the agreement. Not all consulting arrangements are fully successful. Also, unforeseen developments may make continuation of the program unwise or even impossible. If you are required to clear all contractual arrangements with your legal department, they will undoubtedly think of the need to spell out termination arrangements.

Evaluations

It should be made clear that each seminar will require participant evaluations. If you have your own form, you should get agreement on its use. If the consulting firm has its own form, make sure you review it for acceptability. Make sure as well that you will get copies of the evaluations made on the firm's form.

Formalization

Get the consultant to send you a written proposal covering the entire scope of your agreement. A written understanding will help to promote a harmonious consultant-client relationship that is most likely to produce the results you want. It can be disruptive to have disagreements over such things as, for example, who pays freight on educational materials.

The negotiating checklist in Figure 5 has other points to be considered in making arrangements with outsiders. Remember that checklist when your time comes to use outside consultants. If you want to get the most out of the money you spend on training seminars, you will probably, at one time or another, have to supplement your own capabilities with outside assistance. When that time comes for you, go back to this chapter and review the reasons why you might want to use outside resources, what resources are available, what criteria to use in selecting from among them, and what guidelines to consider in negotiating arrangements.

Chapter 5

Developing the Training Plan

Putting on successful seminars requires careful planning, whatever the mix between inside and outside resources. The importance of fact-founded, comprehensive planning is conscientiously preached in virtually all management training courses. But it is not generally practised by training directors. In a limited survey of some 61 training directors in 1979, 21% of the respondents admitted that they had no "written statement of overall purpose or mission" for their departments. Only 15% reported that they had a written plan.*

The arguments in favor of formalized planning are overwhelming. But the practicalities of life in the corporate environment seem to win out over theory. It is difficult to understand why this should be the case. One reason, perhaps, is the need for a clearer, more practical step-by-step approach to the process. If so, this chapter may be of assistance.

---

* Lawrence S. Munson, "Performance Standards: Do Training Directors Practice What They Teach?", *Personnel Journal,* May 1980, pp. 365–367

THE RATIONALE FOR FORMALIZATION

The benefits or advantages of formalized planning are well known and are backed by a good deal of common sense. Notice the use of the word "formalized" in describing planning. Virtually every action of a thinking human being is the result of informal, sometimes almost instantaneous planning. But in management practice it is generally agreed that if a plan is not committed to writing, it is probably not carefully thought out; it certainly cannot be shared by others; and its continuing usefulness is most doubtful.

Better Results

Good planning will usually produce better results. If you stop to think about what you want to accomplish, you are going to take time to consider how important that accomplishment is in your overall area of accountability. Are there other things of greater importance? What is the value of achieving this particular result? How will others in the company look upon its successful achievement? What potential problems are there that could make its accomplishment more difficult or more costly? These are the kinds of questions that you can only consider if you take time to do so. And the time you take will give you greater assurance that the objectives you set will give you the greatest payoff in meaningful results accomplished.

Take, for example, the field sales representative who doesn't take time to plan. He has to drive to a 9:30 A.M. meeting on the other side of town. The non-planning type is late getting up from the breakfast table. He thinks he knows how to get there and can't quickly put his hands on a map of the city to make sure. Time is short so he can't take time to search around the house for it. He rushes out to the car, gets in, and is on his way. Perhaps he is even congratulating himself on the very few minutes he spent between getting up from the breakfast table and shifting into high gear on the way to his appointment.

But, you guessed it, he finds he really doesn't know the way. He doesn't want to take time out to stop and ask directions; but after a few frantic turnbacks, he realizes he has no alternative. It turns out that he has to stop twice to ask directions. As a result, he is twenty minutes late for his meeting and is all tensed up. As a result, he makes a poor presentation. His audience started out annoyed that they had to wait and ends up not accepting his proposal.

Relating this back to the training function, you have to take adequate time to consider and reach conclusions on a range of important questions. What went particularly well last year? Where were opportunities for improvement identified? What training needs did you have to postpone last year, and are they still pressing? What operational, organizational, or technological changes are taking place that could effect the development needs of your clientele? Which of the programs you have had under consideration could have the greatest impact on improving the productivity of human resources in the company? How do your user groups perceive their needs? What are your own capabilities in terms of subject matter competence and seminar leadership skills? To what extent can you anticipate changes in your own staff? The precise questions will differ from one organization to another. But the need to determine what they are and to take time to consider them is universal.

Better Use of Resources

Good planning will not only help you get better results, it will also help you use your resources most efficiently in achieving those results. Planning gives you the time to think through what action steps you have to take, who is going to take these steps, what time frame is involved, and what resources are needed. Frequently, you can identify alternative ways to achieve the results you want. Then, each alternative can be carefully weighed in terms of its possible effect on the quality of the end-result, the degree of risk associated with it, the side-benefits or problems it is likely to produce, and the cost of carrying it through to completion.

The analysis presented in the last chapter illustrates the point. Almost every training director faces this basic question: whether to staff the training function to meet all foreseeable needs, or to use a mixture of internal and external resources and, if so, what mixture. The best answer has to come through thoughtful analysis of each particular situation, and not through intuitive or opportunistic decisions.

Work Made Easier

Good planning makes work easier, a benefit that comes closer to home for the individual manager. If you have a good plan, it becomes a continuing guide to action. You don't have to re-think your options every day. If you have an approved plan, you don't have to re-argue your case, or re-sell your management. It is right there for you and your people to follow.

By way of specific illustration, assume that you have scheduled eight management training seminars in groups of twenty participants over the course of a calendar year. You know that for each seminar there are certain steps that have to be taken and you have determined the lead time for each. You know when to send out reminders and registration forms; when to follow-up by telephone; when to send out materials to the registrants; when to order educational materials; when to reconfirm with the facility; and when to take each of the other steps that might be involved.

The information for each seminar is then posted onto a master calendar. The result is that you know each day of each week exactly what needs to be done and by whom. No fresh problem analysis is involved. No staff meetings have to be taken up by lengthy discussions to untangle problems of coordination. There is a minimum of confusion. It is all laid out for everyone to follow.

Teamwork Encouraged

All the members of your department can function more effectively as a team, because they all know precisely what everyone has to do. If Eleanore's job is to process enrollments that are called in by the various divisions of the company and Eleanore is out sick, someone else can easily step in. The plan has laid out each team member's role and provides a convenient reference if it is necessary to fill in for an absent member.

Basis for Control

Extending the same example, you, as training director, know what has to be done each day. This knowledge is a necessary starting point for making sure it does, in fact, get done. In departments with heavy, ongoing workloads, plans can be broken down into weekly or even daily checklists to provide continuous control. If appropriate, initials can be placed after every item in the checklist to provide an instant reference source for control purposes.

However, there is the danger of over-control. People will tend to be more positively motivated and more productive if they feel they have a degree of freedom in their work. Conversely, they will become frustrated and less productive if they are over-controlled. Finding the right balance is a challenge for the manager. But an acceptable solution is more likely if you have taken the time to think your way through a plan, including thinking about the impact of the plan on your people.

Management theory tells us that without formalized plans, you have no sure basis for knowing whether or not the results you are actually getting are, in fact, acceptable. In such a situation, managers are forced to use their own subjective judgment on the quality of results achieved. They are literally forced to control by personal inspection—injecting themselves into the operations of the department to "check up." This approach, too, will be resented by the people in the department and effect their productivity. Furthermore, the training director's judgment on what is acceptable may differ from that of his or her superior.

Building Support

For a final benefit, the planning process itself gives you the opportunity to get members of higher management involved in the training function, as well as key users of the department's services. Sometimes it is possible to formalize this involvement through a Training Committee or Board of Trustees with membership drawn from top management and higher level executives of user groups.

More and more forward thinking companies are using management training programs as a means of implementing a total, integrated system of management. In such cases, our own experience would strongly support the establishment of a top-level management system committee to oversee the whole process. One of the key responsibilities of such a committee is to contribute to and review the overall management development plan. Top-level management system committees of this type have been used in the past by Union Carbide Corporation (headed by a vice chairman of the board), Merrill Lynch & Co. (also headed by a vice chairman of the board) and Sea-Land Service, Inc. (headed by the then chairman of the board and chief executive officer).

There is a special reason why key users should be included in this planning process. If the operating departments determine the extent to which the training function will be used, then top-level support in these departments is more likely. If you have it, you will fill your seminars. If you don't have it, you may not be able to fill them.

Sometimes there is a further benefit in the involvement of management and users. More people should produce more ideas; and more ideas should result in better plans. But you have to know your own people. It doesn't always work this way. There are some creative thinkers who get keen enjoyment from generating new or different ideas. They can leave you with so many interesting alternatives to research and analyze that the planning process can get bogged down through proliferation. "Just what are all the other companies in the industry doing about this? We really ought to know before we make any final decisions."

PROBLEMS PRESENTED

Along with these benefits, there are a number of constraints that make it difficult to really do a good job. These are the problems that make so many training directors do an incomplete job of planning. It is worth considering each of the more prevalent barriers to planning to determine how valid they really are and what can be done about them.

Time Pressures

First of all, planning takes time—a lot of time—which many training directors have trouble finding. The time you need is not ten minutes here, ten minutes there, and thirty minutes on your commuter train. You have to set aside some solid blocks of hours, which makes it particularly difficult for the training directors who do a good deal of classroom teaching. You can't really do a good job of planning in the late afternoons or evenings after conducting seminars. You're too tired intellectually, and physically as well.

Take the case of a training director in a large insurance brokerage concern. When he first stepped into the job, there were already a large number of training programs in place operating under a training committee that had been established by his predecessor. The new training director had come from a line position and had much to learn. After almost a year in the position, he still hadn't found time to make a needs analysis and develop a plan. He was much too busy carrying out what was already in motion, responding to the requests of his training committee, and learning what he could about the training business.

Organizational Environment

The organizational climate can be another problem. In order to make a thorough needs analysis, you have to involve many other people in the organization. It cannot be done in an ivory tower. The users of the service are probably in the best position to know what's needed— at least they should have some ideas as to what they want. But it is not always possible to get hold of these people. They have many other demands on their time which they may perceive to have a higher priority. If the organization is in a constant state of crisis, or if everyone is shorthanded, it can be practically impossible to get others involved in the planning process.

Top-Level Edicts

Sometimes, unplanned top management actions can keep the training function in a reactive mode, making planning an impossibility. I enjoy telling the story of the company president who attended and was completely carried away by a seminar on human relations, some years ago when this subject was treated somewhat superficially. It is sometimes referred to as the "contented cow" school of human behavior. At any rate, when this president returned to his company after the seminar, the first thing he did was to announce at a staff meeting and follow up by general announcement that every executive, every manager, and every supervisor was required to go through the course.

Almost a year later, the president had an unexpected and not wholly satisfactory opportunity to observe the impact of the course on his people. He came across a foreman in his factory who was holding a worker by the throat and shaking him like a dog would shake a rabbit. Livid with anger, the foreman was shouting, "You did it wrong yesterday and you did it wrong today! If you do it wrong tomorrow, you're fired [long pause] . . . and how's your mother!"

Don't misunderstand me. Top management involvement is to be welcomed. But if the president, or any other powerful top executive, makes a more or less general practice of unanticipated but major demands on the training function, planning becomes academic. In fact, it may become counterproductive. If carefully developed plans have to be abandoned it becomes very frustrating. The more comfortable course is to avoid formal planning altogether and deal with each crisis as it comes along.

User Demands

Another constraint can be the complex of demands from users of the training service. If these demands exceed the capabilities of the training function, planning becomes a matter of priorities. You can argue that the need for planning is greater in this situation—and you're right. But much of the planning has to be done with the active participation of the users, who will have trouble agreeing among themselves on priorities.

Coping with user demands is particularly difficult for new training directors, or, at any rate, those who haven't established a strong position in the organization. They can easily become swamped by the demands for service. In such a position, it is not easy for them to make their own determination of need priorities. It is even more difficult to insist on it.

Budgetary Constraints

The existence of an annual budgetary process forces some kind of planning to take place, but budgetary practices can also be a deterrent to planning in the fullest sense of the word. More often than not, the thinking and analysis that accompany the budgeting process are not recorded in any way. You have a budget, but you have to rely on your memory to recall the reasoning and discussions behind the numbers that are eventually finalized in it. In this way, the budget becomes more useful as a control of expenditures rather than a continuing guide to action.

It is not the budgetary system itself, but the way the system is used that can in some instances be a barrier to effective planning. The problem occurs most frequently on the down side of the business cycle. There may be great uncertainty as to what moneys will be available for training. There may be a good probability that budgeted amounts will be subjected to a series of cutbacks. Training, unfortunately, is usually postponable. Postponing it can boost sagging short-term earnings, but at the expense of neglecting human productivity longer-term.

MAKING THE NEEDS ANALYSIS

The first, and probably the most important, step in developing a training plan is to determine the current and future training needs of the organization. All planning should start with an assessment of the future environment. For the training director, the heart of that environment is the complex of training needs in the organization for all the different population groups to be served.

Methods Available

There are five generally accepted methods for making the needs analysis, each with its own advantages and disadvantages. There are variations on each and sometimes they come in combination. But one thing appears certain, training directors are fully aware of the importance of the needs analysis. They are also acutely aware of some of the practicalities that force some kind of compromise between the ideal and the do-able.

User Requests. The pattern of user requests is by far the most common basis for making a needs analysis. As already noted, user demands can be a constraint on what might be called "full-scope planning." But for many training directors it becomes a realistic basis for determining and projecting training needs. Surely an important measure of success for any training function is the satisfaction of the users of the service that their perceived needs are being met.

In Consolidated Edison of New York City (and many other companies) the training director has review and approval authority over all requests for attendance at outside seminars. This not only helps prevent the company from spending money on marginal or useless seminars; more importantly, it provides inputs on the kind of training that people are seeking. For example, an increasing volume of requests for assertiveness training may suggest establishment of an internal program to meet that need. A control of this kind also prevents line managers from spending money to send people to outside seminars on subjects that are covered in internally provided programs.

Relying on user requests as a basis for establishing training needs is not exactly a scientific method. But it is eminently practical and politically quite safe. The principal negative, if relied on completely, is that the training function is not providing any leadership. It is not anticipating future needs. It is not fulfilling its obligations to the line management team it serves to make sure that the resources committed to training truly get the highest return in terms of improved productivity of human resources.

Representative Committee Judgments. Some training directors organize committees with representatives from different functional and organizational areas as a means for determining training needs. The approach has a great deal to commend it. It is quick and relatively inexpensive, at least in out-of-pocket expenses. It tends to build the support of the line managers represented on the committee and establishes them as positive influence centers throughout the company. It certainly offers a direct channel of communication that makes the training function responsive to the needs of the various elements of the organization.

There are disadvantages, too. There is some loss of control by the training director. A committee can sometimes be carried away by its own presumed expertise and enthusiasm into unsound conclusions. The approach is still not truly fact-founded. It depends more on the subjective judgments of the group. It also tends to create a shared accountability.

A middle road is to make clear that the committee is advisory in nature. The training director is still to be held accountable for the kind and quality of programs and services to be provided, and therefore must have the authority to make the final decisions. A skillful training director can steer the committee away from unwise conclusions and use committee sessions to educate committee members on the training function.

Interviews. A third method, somewhat more time-consuming, is to interview knowledgeable people in different parts of the organization. The interview method gives the training director somewhat greater control, while at the same time having many of the advantages of the representative committee. It provides inputs from many different parts of the organization. For the same reasons mentioned above, it offers the possibility of building support and influence centers in the various user groups.

It takes time, though—a good deal more than the representative committee approach. Then again, its success very much depends on the ability of the training director to find the time to conduct the interviews and to make sure that they are broad-based and representative. Because of the time demands, it is easy to postpone the interviews. There is also some risk of training director bias.

Questionnaires. Questionnaires are potentially the most scientific of the methods reviewed so far. The method can, and probably should, be combined with the interview approach. If the questionnaire is well constructed, the resulting conclusions are likely to be more broadly based and fact-founded than the other methods. At the same time, it does provide for participation.

Shown in Figure 6 is a selected portion of the Allen Management Performance Survey that is used to identify which of the four functions and 19 activities of management have the greatest need for improvement in an organization. The survey is based upon the judgments of a broad spectrum of managers in different levels in the organization as to the kind and quality of management methods actually in use. By analyzing all the responses given to these questions, you can arrive at an index number for each, and compare that number with the average or median scores of hundreds of other companies to determine where the greatest needs might be. The approach gives some quantitative data and comparisons with other companies. It can give a good picture of the management improvement needs of an organization.

Figure 6
EXCERPT FROM THE ALLEN MANAGEMENT PERFORMANCE SURVEY

How often are the following statements true throughout the organization in which you work? "Organization" means the overall organization, including the group in which you work.

- Read the response categories at the right.
- Then circle the number of the response that represents your best judgment.

	Never	Almost Never	Infrequently	About Half the Time	Frequently	Almost Always	Always
1. In this organization, people have clear and reasonable written objectives or goals	0	1	2	3	4	5	6
2. People understand and accept the objectives they are expected to accomplish	0	1	2	3	4	5	6
3. People understand how their own objectives relate to those of the overall organization	0	1	2	3	4	5	6
4. In this organization, before people take action to accomplish their objectives, they state in writing the sequence of steps they will carry out to achieve those objectives	0	1	2	3	4	5	6
5. When people change their objectives, they also change the steps they will take to achieve the objectives	0	1	2	3	4	5	6

	0	1	2	3	4	5	6
6. In this organization, time schedules are used to make sure the work gets done on time	0	1	2	3	4	5	6
7. The schedules are realistic; that is, they can be met if reasonable effort is made	0	1	2	3	4	5	6
8. In this organization, people are required to prepare budgets of the money and other resources required before they are authorized to spend money to carry out projects or programs	0	1	2	3	4	5	6
9. Before people spend money for a program or project, they must show in their budgets that there will be a worthwhile return from the money spent	0	1	2	3	4	5	6
10. People understand and accept the budgets within which they are expected to achieve results	0	1	2	3	4	5	6
11. In this organization, written policies are used to provide people with standing answers to problems that arise repeatedly	0	1	2	3	4	5	6
12. The policies used to give proper consideration of the needs of people	0	1	2	3	4	5	6

This particular survey was conducted in a large commercial bank not too long ago with surprising results. With respect to each of the four functions and the nineteen activities of management, the respondents, managers representing different levels and functions in the bank, indicated that on every one of them the bank compared unfavorably with the companies in the data bank. Needless to say, top management was somewhat disturbed by this poor showing and became more convinced it its own mind of the need for a broad management training program from top to bottom.

The questionnaire approach has some drawbacks, too. It depends rather heavily on the quality of the questionnaire, which in many cases is rather casually constructed. Then again, it is time-consuming. First you have to develop a good questionnaire. In the example just given, it took seven years to remove all of the "bugs" from the detailed questionnaire involved. Then the questionnaires have to be distributed, collected, delinquent respondents contacted, and results summarized. The elapsed time after the questionnaire is developed will at least be many weeks. Furthermore unless supplemented by interviews, it represents one-way communication, with its attendant problems of understanding and interpretation.

Job Requirement Analysis. A fifth method used by Eastman Kodak and Bankers Trust Company, and probably many others, involves a careful analysis of the requirements of each individual position. The method has a much broader focus than identifying training needs. It is typically used to develop a complete system for managing the performance of people. The system requires a determination of the key responsibilities for each job, then for each key responsibility the establishment of standards of performance which are then built into a performance appraisal and counselling system. One of the benefits of the approach is to identify individual training needs, some of which may be common to groups of people. In such a case, a seminar can be set up to meet these needs.

A Recommended Combination

Our recommendation for a practical cost-effective approach is a combination of the questionnaire, interview and representative committee methods whenever a broad survey of needs is to be made, which should be every 2 or 3 years. The job requirements method would appear to be the ideal, but most training directors will have difficulty getting the top management support and resources necessary to carry it out. In between surveys, specific needs will be presented and be proven out from time to time in ways most appropriate to the particular situation. But for a comprehensive survey, here is how we would suggest that it be conducted.

The first step is to consider whether or not to seek outside assistance or do the survey internally. Doing it yourself is less costly and provides a useful opportunity to make meaningful, personal contact with higher management and user groups. On the other hand, a qualified outside resource could free up your own time and possibly provide greater credibility.

If you elect to do it yourself, the next step is to design a questionnaire. It should be structured in such a manner as to give the respondent an understanding of the range of knowledge and skills to be considered and an easy way to differentiate priorities. Both of these features can be served by providing a more-or-less complete checklist with a priority code. This design has the further advantage of easy statistical summarization. At the same time, some open-end questions can help avoid too tight a structure, which could discourage independent thought. In setting up your checklist, make sure you are providing the means for determining the differing needs of different population groups. You need to differentiate between those groups concerned primarily with technical skills and those with management skills. The latter category needs to be further broken down by management level, as for example: (1) presupervisory, (2) supervisory, (3) managers, and (4) executives. Before going ahead with your questionnaire, you should involve your training committee. Give them an opportunity to contribute to its design and make suggestions on its use.

Third, you have to select the population to be surveyed, and provide them with the questionnaire and covering memorandum of explanation and instructions. Since we recommend follow-up interviews, we suggest the number of respondents be not too large. Otherwise, you are imposing a heavy interview schedule on yourself. But before you cut back too far on the size of the respondent group, keep in mind that each interview can be an opportunity to build understanding and support for the training function.

The next step is to follow up and interview the respondents. Although not absolutely necessary, personal meetings will prove much more effective than telephone discussions. The questionnaires should be completed by the respondents before the interview, but should be finalized during the interview. Changes may need to be made as a result of the exchange of views. Try to be a prober and a listener during these meetings. You want to get the ideas of the respondents. You will be more successful in doing so if you give the appearance of being sincerely interested in their opinions.

After you have had a chance to evaluate the questionnaires and interviews, you will want to review your findings with your training committee. At this point in the process you are not yet concerned about funding, but only about getting some sense of agreement on the kind of training needs identified and their relative priorities.

THE TRAINING PLAN

Although the primary focus of this book is on training seminars, the needs analysis and the training plan to be developed from it will be broader in scope. But even then, seminars will represent a major portion of the plan.

As we mentioned earlier, most training directors will make some form of a needs analysis; but most of them do not build this needs analysis into a formal, comprehensive training plan. The arguments favoring formalized planning are strong, but the practical barriers that stand in the way seem to prevail in actual practice. In an effort to encourage more training directors to overcome these barriers, here are some specific suggestions on how a practical and useful training plan can be developed.

General Guidelines

First, there are a number of general guidelines for an acceptable training plan. The form that any particular training plan will take is subject to individual preferences. But in any event these fundamentals should be followed.

Clearly Needs Related. The heart of the training plan should be the needs analysis. The objectives in the plan should be clearly traceable to defined needs. It is axiomatic that any service rendered should meet the needs of the users if it is worth providing at all. Since you probably won't be able to fund all the identified needs in the forthcoming budget year, you can still focus attention on the remaining needs by including them in the plan for future years.

Experience Based. The plan should reflect an analysis of actual experience. The fact that a given program is getting an excellent reception is an important consideration in determining whether to continue it. If another program has turned up with some problems, the plan may call for some program redesign or perhaps for discontinuance. You can learn a great deal from actual experience. What you learn is an essential frame of reference in planning for the future and should be directly reflected in the plan.

Assumptions. Early in your planning, collect whatever assumptions as to future conditions and events may be appropriate to the particular situation. For example, if a relatively sharp rate of growth is expected for a number of years into the future, an increasing demand for management training might be expected. New management positions will have to be established and the total management population increased. Another example might be changing computer technology that could require retraining of a significant population. Almost inevitably, whether explicitly stated or not, assumptions have to be made as to the scale of effort in training that the corporation will be willing to fund.

Measurable Objectives. The plan being developed should provide for two kinds of objectives. There should be broad objectives covering the overall program for the time period involved. There should also be specific, behavioral objectives for each of the separate programs included in the plan. These objectives should be accompanied by measurable standards. In this way, the results to be accomplished can be much more clearly visualized by all at the outset; and their degree of actual attainment is less affected by differences in subjective viewpoint.

Examples of the first type of objective might be to develop a revised first-level supervisory training program; to provide a two-day workshop in performance counseling to assist in the effective implementation of a new performance appraisal system; or to establish a capability to measure more accurately the impact on the job of certain ongoing programs.

Examples of the second type of objective might be:

1. To enable each participant to develop and refine an action plan for solving a significant problem or taking advantage of a special opportunity actually faced on the job;

2. To enable each participant to apply the company's performance evaluation system successfully in appraising performance and coaching of immediate subordinates;

3. To enable each participant to provide relevant information on all the company's products and to apply the company's established sales techniques and procedures.

The Seminar Schedule. Backing up these objectives should be a listing of the seminars that are scheduled, together with the time and place of each offering. In order to facilitate registrations, you should publish a separate promotional piece describing each of the seminars in terms of behavioral objective, subject matter, methodology, and cost, if any, for the registrants. The piece can then be made an appendix to the training plan.

Coverage. The population to be reached and the subject matter to be provided to them should be clearly indicated in the plan. If appropriate, priorities can be indicated in the event a cut-back in funds is a possibility. Use of a priority system could introduce a degree of flexibility into the budget that is useful in making a quick response to changing business conditions.

Coordination. The formalization of the plan provides an opportunity to secure the participation of user groups and top management. Getting these people to "sign off" on the plan can save many problems later. They are not likely to attack it, for example, as not being responsive to their needs or lacking innovation. Putting it more positively, proper coordination creates a much more favorable climate in which to conduct the training seminars.

Time Span. Training plans should extend longer than a single year. Successive one-year planning is too short-sighted. Training needs do not fit nicely into one-year packages. For example, management training requires a series of iterations over the active working span of a manager for the greatest impact. Furthermore, budgetary constraints may require postponement of certain portions of training to future years.

Cost-Effectiveness. Every plan should include some estimate of its overall value or benefit and the cost of its implementation. Estimating costs is usually not too difficult. Relating these costs to value received or overall benefit is almost always difficult and often not done at all. "Costs" includes more than budgeted expenditures. The training department may have a budget consisting of the salaries and fringe benefits of its assigned people, some allowance for consulting assistance, and further appropriations for such matters as seminar facilities, travel, and the like. The true costs of the training plan, on the other hand, should include the cost of travel and maintenance for participants in the scheduled seminars. For most companies, this can be a very substantial amount indeed, even though it may show up elsewhere in the company budget. However, the salary expense of participants for time away from their jobs should not be included. When people are hired for positions in an organization it is understood that part of their ongoing employment will be dedicated to training, just as an allowance is made for vacations and sickness.

It is in trying to place a value on the benefits of the plan that the greater difficulties arise. Managers as a whole have been so "brain washed" by the accounting profession that they are very loathe to make any quantitative estimate of benefit if it has to rest on assumptions. This is not meant as a criticism. The discipline provided to us by the accounting profession is of great value. But in this one respect, it may be unnecessarily inhibiting. For example, a conservative—hence acceptable—assumption on getting sales trainees out in the field productively selling one or two weeks sooner can, in some businesses, be directly translated into added revenue and profit. Or again, a conservative assumption on productivity gain can also be translated into added profit. In either case, value assumptions provide a better frame of reference for getting agreement that the plan is really worth doing.

Suggested Format

There are many acceptable formats for a good training plan. The subject is wide open to individual preferences, but we suggest in Figure 7 a broad outline that can serve as a starting point or frame of reference—particularly for those training directors who have no precedents from which to work. A good framework doesn't necessarily mean a good plan. But it does provide a "track to run on" that should facilitate good planning. And good planning means more than a needs analysis, although that is well recognized to be of paramount importance.

Figure 7
TRAINING PLAN FORMAT

1. *OVERVIEW.* A brief summary of the plan, assumptions made, populations to be reached, subject matter to be presented, and any newsworthy aspects.

2. *OBJECTIVES.* A reminder as to the basic mission of the training department; delineation of specific objectives for the planning period; and specification of the behavioral objective for each course being offered.

3. *STANDARDS.* List the performance measurements that will determine if each overall training objective and each course objective has been successfully achieved.

Figure 7 (*Continued*)

4. *VALUATION OR BENEFITS.*   Include some estimate of the impact or benefits to be achieved. If done carefully, this can be a good selling tool.

5. *PROGRAM AND SCHEDULE.*   The main portion of the plan should provide programming and scheduling back-up for each departmental objective and each separate training program. For each seminar scheduled there should be a short summary of subject matter, target population group, background of the scheduled seminar leader, location, dates, fee—if any—and method of registration. An option is to attach a brochure describing the seminars offered as an attachment or appendix.

6. *BUDGET.*   This section should contain a consolidation and appropriate breakdowns of the expenses involved in each aspect of the plan.

7. *EVALUATION.*   Outline here the methods to be employed in determining whether training objectives set in the plan are in fact achieved.

Chapter 6
Seminar Design

How much of the success of a seminar is due to the material, and how much is due to the seminar leader? This is a question that experienced seminar leaders frequently ask themselves. The answers they provide will probably vary widely. One quite successful professional in the field, when asked this question answered, "80% is the material, 20% is the seminar leader."

Although opinions will differ on the exact proportion, most professionals, if pressed on the subject, would agree that the design of the seminar is clearly of primary importance. Putting it another way, with good material an average performer can be quite successful. With poor material, even the most highly skilled professional will have trouble pulling off the seminar. The way a poorly designed seminar has to be saved, is for the presenter to make impromptu changes in response to the reactions of the participant group, which means it comes back to seminar design.

A good working knowledge of seminar design will prove useful in several ways. The most important one is in the development of a new seminar. Even if someone else is developing it for you, you have to be able to evaluate the end result. Other ways that a knowledge of seminar design will be useful are in redesigning an existing seminar, or evaluating a program that may be offered to you. All the training seminars that you sponsor have to rest on a sound design in order to be most effective.

THE SEMINAR OBJECTIVE

The starting point in seminar design is to define your objective. What are you trying to accomplish, and for what population group? Are you trying to train certain operators to become skilled on some new equipment, to provide a refresher course in management skills to experienced middle-managers, or to improve the communication skills of sales representatives? You have to know your training objective and target population group.

The reasons you should define your seminar objective clearly are fundamental. Without such a definition, you have no sure basis for determining subject matter content and educational approach. If the participant group does not consider the subject matter relevant to their needs, you are not going to be successful. The participants will not respond to the material presented and won't show the improved performance on the job that you are trying to secure. Furthermore, you have to know your target population group to design the proper educational approach. If your approach is too simple for the group, it could easily frustrate and irritate them. If too sophisticated, they may not follow the flow of ideas and not learn from the seminar.

To be more specific, you have to determine the degree of skill orientation as compared to theory. Although improved performance on the job may be the objective of most training seminars, sometimes there is a heavy overtone of general education for purposes of perspective and broad understanding. Some of the better known programs for top executives have a very strong orientation away from specific skill building and toward creative thinking or philosophic concepts.

You can carry the analysis a step further and identify different categories of objectives. The principal focus in this book is individual behavior change on the job. But there may be other objectives. Awareness may be the principal objective in certain safety training programs. Sometimes the focus is on changing the behavior of an entire organizational unit—or a total enterprise. In each case, the objective would have significant impact on the design of the program.

This line of thinking underlines the importance of the training plan. If you have developed a comprehensive training plan, it will already have defined the behavorial objective of the seminar to be developed and the target population. If you have no training plan you have to go to your needs analysis, which should delineate the objective and the target group. If you are lacking both a training plan and a needs analysis, your first step in seminar design is to determine precisely what the objective is and for what population group.

SUBJECT MATTER CONTENT

Once the objective and the population group have been clearly defined, the overall subject matter content should become clear. Nevertheless, there are a number of factors to consider with respect to the subject matter and how it is treated in the seminar.

Scope and Depth

Although the depth and breadth of subject matter treatment will be largely determined by the needs analysis and the stated objective, other considerations should be reviewed. For example, if the target population is not truly homogeneous, then the subject matter will have to be structured to take into account the different levels of understanding and sophistication that will be encountered. You may need to provide a "fast track" and a "slow track." Core material may have to be supplemented by optional team exercises.

Constraints of time can also affect subject matter treatment. You may be limited for practical reasons to a three-day configuration, regardless of the scope and complexity of the subject matter. If so, you need to consider more extensive reading assignments before the seminar and in the evenings. Matters of lesser priority may have to be covered by lecture or group discussion instead of through work exercises.

Quality of Material

For the seminar to be truly cost effective, you have to bring to bear the best and most appropriate subject matter material available. In some instances this will be a greater problem than it is in others. In the field of human behavior, for example, there are many well-respected theories, and new insights are continuously being developed. It is difficult to make valid judgments as to relative quality. At the other extreme is training operators in some new equipment or system supplied by a vendor. If a reputable vendor supplies the training program, you can usually be sure of the quality of the material.

Sequence

Learning is greatly facilitated if the subject matter is presented in a logical, easy-to-follow flow of ideas. The process should begin by providing a proper frame of reference, and then proceed from one idea to the next in a logical sequence that builds one idea upon the other much as a bricklayer goes about building a wall, one brick at a time. The participants should be provided with something familiar and well understood to which they can relate each new idea as it comes along. The best way to get a logical sequence is to develop an expanded outline of the ideas to be presented in the seminar. Then, test the logic of your outline by presenting it orally to someone else—or to your image in a mirror if no one else is available. First, you need to get the broad structure. The details can be filled in later.

When McKinsey and Company first started recruiting associates directly from graduate business schools, the management group of the firm was very surprised to discover that top graduates from the most distinguished educational institutions could not write an acceptable business report. They had to be put through an intensive course in report writing. The central focus of the course was the need for a single theme or "angle," and structuring the ideas or proof necessary to establish this theme in a preliminary outline composed of complete sentences. The same is true in developing an effective training seminar. The "theme" is the behavioral objective and the outline simplifies the design process.

Interfaces

In building the subject matter around this expanded outline, you have to be aware of interfaces with other programs and existing practices in order to avoid possible confusion or resistance. The bitter experience of a project manager of a large management development program for a major department in an eastern state is a sad example of such a conflict. In the second year of this program, he brought in a second outside vendor with impeccable credentials, and attempted to introduce portions of an established, off-the-shelf program provided by that vendor. Unfortunately, the vocabulary and approach provided by the second vendor contradicted in some very important respects that which had already been provided to the target population the year before by the first vendor. It was very embarassing to all concerned when the first group refused to go along with the second vendor's program. The group was supposedly being trained to conduct the program, but the seminar leaders-to-be knew they would not be able to present it successfully to their peers because of the conflicts and confusion.

GENERAL DESIGN CONSIDERATIONS

In developing the full seminar from the expanded outline, you need to be aware of some general design considerations that come into play regardless of the subject matter. It is useful to review these briefly before dealing with the development of participant materials and materials for the seminar leader.

Proven Learning Process

A proven, adult learning process should be followed. But it should not be followed with such unvarying precision as to be monotonous. A few years ago, I audited a seminar leader who failed to observe this caution. At eight different points in the 3-day management seminar, he was required to present a set of management principles, each set covering a different aspect of management. Being given some leeway on how to do it, he elected to treat each set of principles in exactly the same way. He assigned a principle to each of a number of teams of two or three participants, asking them to restate it in their own words and supply an example or illustration of how a manager could use the principle on the job. The technique itself is not a bad one. It provides for some interaction in small groups. It tests understanding and gets some degree of simulated application. But because it was done the same way every time, the group came to expect it and got bored with it. "Oh, not again!" they would say, as he continued on his enthusiastic way.

There appears to be no unanimity as to the most effective learning process. Some educators strongly favor the case method, getting participants to draw conclusions from some situation presented to them. My own experience in management training suggests that this is an effective approach with more experienced groups who have some background to draw upon. It can also be used as a change of pace. But for most groups I can suggest a six-step method that begins with motivation and continues through to providing feedback on application of the ideas being presented.

1. Motivation. The first step in this learning process is to secure a positive, motivational attitude. The participants should be made to see how they could benefit personally from learning and using

the ideas and information to be presented. They have to be made to see the relevance of each idea as it comes along.

2. Explanation. Then the ideas should be presented clearly, and in a logical sequence so the process of learning can begin.

3. Demonstration. To get greater and clearer understanding, the seminar leader can do or perform that which is to be learned, or provide an example or illustration to demonstrate the idea.

4. Self-Evaluation. The participants should then be given an opportunity to assess their own understanding of the materials presented. For example, you can use a self-evaluation worksheet. Or you can plan for the seminar leader to use test questions in a group discussion.

5. Application. The learners should then have an opportunity to apply the ideas in application exercises, cases, or—ultimately— on the job.

6. Feedback. The participants need to have some way of knowing whether they are performing properly. Without feedback, they cannot know what they are doing right that should be continued and what they are doing wrong that should be discontinued. The design should provide for this needed feedback.

Duration

Although much depends on the subject matter to be covered, three days appears to be widely accepted as a good time period. But four and even five days may be desirable in special cases. For example: intensive training in professional management concepts and methods is difficult to accomplish in three days. Many companies prefer to extend it for a fourth or even a fifth day. On the other hand, a narrowly focused program on, say, performance counseling can be effectively performed in a single day, or perhaps two days.

Daily Schedule

There are no clear-cut answers on what is the best daily schedule. A lot depends upon the previous experience and traditions of the particular organization, which is another way of saying the expectations of the participants. Here are some helpful hints distilled from practical experience:

Starting Time. If the seminar is set in a hotel and the group is living in, you can start as early as 8:00 A.M. or even 7:30, which is when most people are more alert. How early you can start may depend on how early and how efficiently breakfast is being served. On the other hand, if there are a large number of commuters, you probably have to conform to their accustomed time schedule. It is sometimes wise to let the group have some leeway in setting their own starting time. The payoff for an earlier start is earlier adjournment.

Breaks. Regardless of starting time, you should limit each learning (and sitting) period to roughly one hour, with two breaks in the morning and two in the afternoon. Ten minutes ought to be long enough for a break. But sometimes, you may have to provide an opportunity to make telephone calls. In this case, one break can be lengthened and the other shortened.

Lunch. Group luncheons will facilitate discussion and interaction around the subject matter covered that morning. They also take up less time. Scheduling luncheons cannot easily be built into the design of the program, since much depends upon the efficiency of the dining room or restaurant. One hour is usually sufficient, but you can't be sure. The presenter of the program can always make variations in particular cases.

Adjournment. Seminars should be set to allow at least six and no more than seven solid hours of classroom time, exclusive of breaks and lunches. There is a limit to what even a dedicated group can sit and absorb. In effect, therefore, the adjournment time is set by the starting time. Almost invariably, creative thinkers in the group will come up with suggestions designed to provide for earlier adjournment on the last day. Sometimes it is to have a special session the night before. Other times it is to start earlier or go straight through lunch. These ideas have to be left to the tact and good judgment of the seminar leader.

Evening Assignments. Evening reading assignments have the advantage of reducing the amount of straight explanation or lecture on the succeeding day. For live-in participants, team exercises or cases will heighten interest levels and help keep the fun-lovers out of mischief. Be careful that these are not too onerous, or available recreation facilities will represent a frustration rather than an opportunity for a change of pace. Our preference is *not* to schedule formal sessions involving the entire group. After a long day already, the participants will not function efficiently—particularly if the facility is promoting a "happy hour" before dinner, with two drinks for the price of one. On longer seminars, one completely free evening will be appreciated.

PARTICIPANT INVOLVEMENT

The more you can induce participants to share ideas and experiences with each other, the greater the level of participant interest and commitment. Periods of straight lecture should be limited to no more than ten minutes at a time. Even then, the presentation should be punctuated by lively examples and humorous asides. Here are some ways to secure participant involvement.

Pre-seminar Assignments

Pre-seminar assignments have a number of important advantages, if they are designed skillfully and the participants really carry them out. The danger is that there will be a wide range of commitment levels. A few people will do them so thoroughly that they may dominate the group discussion at the seminar. Others less committed may be left behind, if the pace is set to accommodate the higher level of preparation. If the pace is set for the poorly prepared, the few well-prepared may become bored. For most groups the advantages of pre-seminar assignments outweigh these minor considerations.

Raising Knowledge Levels. One advantage is that advance reading assignments can raise the knowledge level of participants and thus reduce the need for lecture during the seminar itself. If lecture time can be reduced, the time available for interaction between and among the participants can be increased.

Establishing Relevance. Also, requiring participants to relate text knowledge in the pre-seminar reading assignments to their own jobs can make the seminar appear more immediately relevant and useful. This is not only a good form of involvement, but it also builds a positive motivation to learn.

Building Expectations. Requiring participants to write down their expectations for the forthcoming seminar produces a third advantage: it helps to build anticipation and interest level. It has the further advantage of giving the seminar presenter the opportunity to make sure that these expectations are not at variance with the program to be presented. Setting this matter straight at the outset can avoid disappointments and frustrations.

Pre-seminar Needs Analysis

Another technique to raise the level of participant involvement is the pre-seminar needs analysis. It can be in the form of self-assessment, through a check list or questionnaire, or it can be an assessment by superior, subordinates, and peers. If the evaluations of others run sharply counter to the participant's own self-evaluation, the discrepancy can be quite an eye-opener. This revelation can add a sense of special urgency to those parts of the seminar that can help to overcome these identified shortcomings. Regardless of method, the net result should be to identify for the participant specific areas of need, and heighten expectation and interest when those areas are treated in the seminar.

"Ice-Breakers"

At the very start of the seminar, an exercise to break inhibitations and encourage participation is most useful. One easy "ice-breaker" is to divide the group into teams of two, each interviewing the other for 5 minutes to get the information necessary to introduce the other to the entire group. This exercise works best if the presenter challenges the participants to be "probing reporters" and to find some especially newsworthy aspect of each other's background. It is somewhat time consuming. But it is an easy way for strangers to get acquainted and a good way to get them accustomed to taking active roles in the seminar.

Group Discussion

Sharing of ideas and information through group discussion can be a useful device throughout the seminar. The discussion can be started through questions posed by the seminar leader or come about as a result of reports made by team leaders after team exercises and case assignments. In designing the seminar, the seminar leader should be provided with suggested questions that will induce lively exchange of ideas. If the questions are backed up by "anticipated responses," it is easier for the leader to draw out the group or supply any important, missing ideas.

Application Exercises

Relating freshly learned ideas to structured problems or assignments is a necessary part of the adult learning process. It is most effectively done in subgroups or teams, but can be done individually. Assignments can be made to teams of two or three who can form groups without leaving their places in the seminar. For larger teams, "break-away" tables—or even rooms—are preferable to rearranging chairs to form groups at or near the participants assigned seminar places. The teams, ideally, should not be larger than five members each. If a team gets too large, it is easy for individual team members to take an inactive role. On the other hand, individual work exercises can be useful in trying to relate classroom subject matter to the participant's own job. But they have the distinct disadvantage of no group interaction. A heavy silence settles over the group. If it lasts too long, your group lose some rapport and commitment.

Cases

Well-designed cases, which are less structured and longer than application exercises, can also stimulate active discussion, especially if strong and differing viewpoints are developed. This result will show up in the subgroups and later, when these groups are reconvened, will animate the group as a whole. Again, you should keep the subgroups down to five or less members to encourage involvement and interaction. Typically, the group is asked to select a leader who will report back the conclusions of the subgroup to the group as a whole.

Games

Computer-assisted instruction is making competitive games an increasingly popular and powerful avenue of learning. Although time-consuming, games have the potential for deep participant involvement because of the competition that can be generated among teams. Sometimes, a form of competition can be induced by assigning the same question on a case to two teams at the same time, with the second team assigned to challenge or add to the first team's answer, and the first team given the opportunity for rebuttal. Another variation of the game theme is the "great debate," in which different sides of an issue are assigned to different teams. Each team is asked to make the strongest possible case for its side of the issue.

In one popular management seminar, the seminar leader gets the participants as a group to critique the "action plan," developed by each of several individual participants. After trying a number of different approaches, one leader reported that group discussion was considerably enhanced by making a game of the process. Teams of four or five are established, and given names after well-known professional ball teams: Cardinals, Angels, Brewers and Yankees (or other teams for other seasons). Points are awarded to the teams for valid observations made by its members and a good deal of friendly rivalry develops.

Role Playing

Asking participants to assume certain "roles" is another popular means for getting involvement. With videotape feedback, role playing can be a very stimulating, even dramatic way of learning. However, it is time-consuming. The greatest overall involvement takes place if it is enacted in small teams. However, there are potential disadvantages. The seminar leader rarely has an opportunity to provide feedback to the players in the small group environment. On the other hand, if role playing is done in the group as a whole, only a few individuals get the benefit of active participation.

Role playing has its most important place in seminars that are intended to develop specific skills in the participants. When accompanied by skillful feedback, role playing, or "behavior modeling" as it is often termed in these seminars, is an effective means for developing proficiency in such activities as interviewing, on-the-job coaching, selling, or performance counselling—to name just a few.

PARTICIPANT MATERIALS

The seminar designer ultimately ends up with two sets of end-product materials: materials for the participants and materials for the seminar leader. Let's first review the materials for the participants. Those going through the seminar need written materials that clearly explain and illustrate the ideas presented in the program. The materials also provide a continuing reference source. Usually these educational materials will contain a text outline of the subject matter. As appropriate, there might also be background information for work exercises and role playing, worksheets to be used in team or individual work assignments, cases, logic diagrams or models, and other visualizations.

Types

Generally, there are four types of written materials for seminar participants, which are frequently used in combination with each other. Each has its own particular advantages and limitations. To some degree, the choice is influenced by the past experience of the leader and the expectations of the participants.

Outlines and Worksheets. One approach to educational materials is a simple topic outline—with ample space for note-taking. It is quick, easy and inexpensive. But it is probably the least effective organizational aid. The method can be quite effective for other purposes (for example, discussion of important issues in a staff meeting or conference), but in a seminar situation, it offers little to assist the learning process—except to encourage the kind of extreme note-taking that can impede the learning process.

Textbooks. Text material, hard or soft cover, is most frequently and appropriately used for pre-seminar or evening reading assignments. Advance text assignments make it possible to reduce the amount of lecture in the seminar to a minimum. Evening reading assignments can be used for the same purpose: reducing lecture periods on the following day. Texts can also be used as a means of reviewing the material covered previously. Finally, textbooks are most useful as a continuing reference, much more so than the other participant materials.

Workbooks. By far the most common and probably the most useful learning aid is the participant's workbook designed to be used actively during the course of the seminar. A workbook lends itself well to a variety of materials: subject matter outline, background material for team exercises, worksheets for individual work exercises, cases, diagrams, models, and other forms of visualizations. Workbooks should be logically structured with an easy-to-follow sequence. Clearly stated behavioral objectives and tabs to divide the work into logical segments contribute to the effectiveness of the workbook.

Handouts. The easiest way to adapt standard educational materials to different groups is the use of handouts as substitutes or supplements for workbook pages. This technique is also useful for providing examples of acceptable solutions to application problems or for providing tailored illustrations or examples of subjects covered in the seminar. However, too many handouts at the same time can be confusing. And the seminar leader can get confused too, handing out the wrong papers or in the wrong sequence.

Design Options

Participant materials can be assembled or packaged in a variety of ways. The simpler, less expensive techniques are recommended for special, non-recurring seminars. The more elaborate, expensively bound type of materials are appropriate for seminars to be given to large populations. Nevertheless there are options.

Bound. A more-or-less permanent cover, usually paperbound soft-back is typically used for textbooks or for booklets provided with standard off-the-shelf modular programs. The rationale is that no change is expected in the materials for a long period of time and they will be used by large populations. Bound materials are used by outside vendors for another reason: they provide better copyright protection.

Loose Leaf. Three-hole-punched pages in a loose leaf binder are by far the most popular design for participant workbooks. They are widely used both for internally developed workbooks and for those provided and conducted by outside firms. The loose leaf format offers a great deal of flexibility. Additions and eliminations are more easily made if a page numbering system is adopted that starts each segment off with a new sequence. The materials can be easily changed either to update them or adapt them to different participant groups. If handout material is pre-punched, it can be inserted into the workbook for safekeeping and future reference.

Loose Pages. Loose pages are typically associated with handouts. But sometimes loose pages are provided already assembled in folders. This technique can be useful, if different sized materials are used. For example, often materials produced for other purposes are brought together for a particular meeting. As an expediency, or a last-minute exercise, loose pages are a way to pull some things together quickly and offer great flexibility. However, loose pages are not easily usable for preseminar assignments nor for postseminar reference.

Frequent Problems

No matter what type of participant materials are used, there are some problems that may be encountered. The reader can probably supply many more than I will mention here, but these seem to be the ones I meet most frequently.

The Sequence of Materials. One of these problems centers on the proper location of work exercises and cases. Should these be interleaved with the course outline or put separately in an appendix? Or should there be some combination of the two? In my experience, participants favor interleaving these materials so that ideas and applications follow in consecutive sequence. To give them greater latitude and flexibility in conducting the seminar, seminar leaders, on the other hand, like to have case materials in the appendix together with other, optional materials.

The experience of the seminar leader and the degree of homogeneity in the participant groups often determine how material sequences are best arranged. If the target population is quite homogeneous and the seminar leader not particularly experienced, preserving the sequence is preferable because omissions and additions are not desired. The same is true if a large number of seminar leaders have been recruited to put on a particular program for a large population. The way to make sure that all of the participants get essentially the same learning experience is to structure the seminar tightly and discourage variations. On the other hand, if the participant groups are expected to bring in a variety of levels of sophistication or experience, and if the seminar leader is a true professional, then the cases and work exercises should be put in the appendix. Such an arrangement gives the leader the greatest flexibility to select those materials in the back of the workbook that are relevant and interesting to each group. Such a tailored approach requires experience, insight, and flexibility.

Use of "Suggested Solutions." In the learning process, there are times when it may be useful to provide participants with suggested solutions to certain problems they have been given. But my experience suggests that these solutions should not be put in the workbook. Once the pattern is revealed, the more alert participants will learn to page their way forward in the workbook to find the suggested solutions. In this way, the suggested solutions give these participants an excuse to avoid thinking the problems through for themselves. An easy solution denies them the benefit of the learning experience.

Improvements. A large number of continuing, minor improvements can easily create internal inconsistencies between workbooks, text, and audio/visual aids that were originally fully coordinated. The temptation to "tinker" can be extraordinarily strong. My suggestion is to accumulate minor improvements and then make fewer but more extensive revisions. At the time of these revisions, ample allowance should be made for careful editing to ensure consistency between all of the different seminar materials, for both the participants and leaders.

Production Mistakes. If one or maybe several participants have defective or incorrect workbooks, it can be very disconcerting for a seminar leader. Usually the problem involves incorrect pages, pages omitted, or pages unnecessarily duplicated. Sometimes a defective binder mechanism can be the problem. Such problems are even more likely to occur during the transition from an older to a newer set of participant materials.

There are preventive measures. If practicable, the seminar leader can double check the participant materials before the seminar starts and take corrective action if defects are discovered. If time or circumstances do not permit this, then a useful precaution is to have several extra sets of participant materials on hand that can be quickly and easily substituted for the defective ones.

LEADER'S MATERIALS AND AIDS

As important as the participant materials in seminar design, is the development of materials and visual aids needed by the seminar leader. Broadly speaking, these materials fall into two categories: the leader's guide and audio-visuals. On the horizon are computer terminals as a further assist to the leader and training will shortly necessitate "courseware" (software for the course). Here I will confine the discussion to the essentials. The leader's guide provides a road map or detailed schedule for the leader to follow in conducting the seminar. The audio-visuals provide various kinds of visualizations, sometimes accompanied by sound, to be used with the participants to reinforce the learning process.

Leader's Guides

There are several ways to arm the seminar leader with the necessary guidelines. At one extreme are detailed, formalized leader's guides. At the other extreme is a brief outline of topics for each day with suggested time schedules. In the initial design of a seminar, the more complete, formal approach is essential. But as seminar leaders become familiar with the seminar and subject matter, they tend to develop their own guides of a much more informal and summary type.

Formal, Detailed Guides. In the initial design, or any major revision of a seminar, the more detailed, formal leader's guide is a necessity. Typically such a leader's guide will include the following:

1. A pre-seminar check list.
2. The behavioral objective for the whole seminar and for each segment.
3. A summary overview of each segment.

4. A prescribed sequence of subject matter—with suggested time schedule.

5. Suggested remarks for the seminar leader to: introduce the program, introduce each day, and bridge each subject transition.

6. Audio/visual material cues.

7. Suggested questions and anticipated responses for leading group discussions.

8. Suggested solutions for application exercises and cases.

9. Evening assignments.

Informal Leader's Guides. The formal guide is usually replaced by some personalized, informal system, once a leader becomes trained in a seminar and fully knowledgable in its subject matter. The formal leader's guide becomes too detailed and bulky for the experienced presenter. It is much easier to develop a shorter, summary version, which comes in many forms to suit individual preferences but should always be within the parameters of the instructional design.

One technique is the use of cue cards. The cards can be in the 5x8 or 3x5 inch size. The cards can be used inconspicuously and can easily be revised. Cards also take up very little space and can quickly be resequenced. You are in deep trouble if you lose individual cards, or if you can't put a complete thought on a single card. But if you feel more comfortable using cue cards, go right ahead.

Another technique is to put crib notes on the frames of overhead projector transparencies. It is a convenient and unobservable technique, particularly for comments planned in elaboration of the subject matter of the transparency. It cannot be used as a complete guide because the notes will be tied to specific visuals. But it can be a useful adjunct to some other method.

Another device is the use of a broad felt-tipped pen, or equivalent, on full page-size paper. This offers the advantage of being able to write your notes more boldly because there is more room to do so. As a result, you can place your outline on the leader's table and read it from a distance of several feet away. The individual pages can be three-hole punched and placed inconspicuously within the pages of a participant workbook. Changes are easy to make by obliterations and additions to individual "master" pages, which can then be photocopied.

For the professional, thoroughly familiar with the seminar, a brief outline of topics for the day and scheduled times may be sufficient. But heed this word of caution! It is easy to become overconfident.

For example, a very experienced seminar leader was embarking on the subject of motivation and human behavior when his mind suddenly went blank. Momentarily, he was at a loss whether to accredit Theory X and Theory Y to Hertzberg or McGregor. My recommendation is to err on the side of preparation. Have all of the specifics readily available in case *your* mind goes blank.

Audio/Visual Aids

In addition to the leader's guide, the seminar design must include the use of some form of audio/visual reinforcement. Technology and techniques are changing in this field, but there are a variety of audio/visual aids currently in common use. Each offers benefits and advantages, but each has its limitations.

The Overhead Projector. The most widely used visual aid is the overhead projector. It has a number of advantages. It has great versatility and definition, and can be operated by the seminar leader from the podium. There is usually no need to dim the normal lighting in the room. Direct eye contact with the participants is maintained. Presenters easily can change the sequence of transparencies, or return to one previously shown. And blank, acetate sheets can be used to write on or to record comments from the class.

These practical advantages outweigh the relatively few shortcomings of overhead projectors. But for the record, here are its demerits: first, the image projected on the screen will be larger (hence wider) at the top than at the bottom—the "Keystone" effect—unless an attachment is used to tip the top of the screen forward. Second, it is sometimes difficult to get the image level on the screen, either because one side of the projector needs to be elevated or because the transparencies are placed carelessly on the equipment. Third, for very large groups some overhead projectors won't throw a large enough image as sharply or as conveniently as 35mm equipment. Fourth, the upright arm can interfere with the vision of some participants, unless it can be folded down when not in use. Use of models without this fold-down arm feature means that the total projector has to be removed from the leader's table if 35mm slides are also being used, to prevent interference with the image projected by the other equipment. On balance, however, the overhead is a satisfactory technical aid.

The 35mm Projector. A 35mm slide projector equipped with a carousel slide holder is another popular aid. It provides a superior image, can be used with small or very large groups, and involves little production expense to shoot and reproduce the slides. Moreover, it offers more opportunity to use photographs of people and places, a technique not as easily introduced on the overhead projector. But there are some drawbacks. The machine has to be operated at a distance from the seminar leader's table, which requires either an extension to the control cord or an expensive projection booth and remote control equipment. Sequencing is inflexible, except with expensive equipment. The seminar leader has to have a method of keeping track of what slides are coming up next. Furthermore, room lights usually have to be dimmed to get the sharpest image. If this requires constant running back and forth to a light switch on the wall, it can be both bothersome and disconcerting. Sometimes there is no middle ground because of the lighting system available in the seminar room. You either have to have too much light or virtually none at all. The latter situation makes it difficult for participants to take notes (and easier to sneak in a short nap!).

The 35mm projector is often used in conjunction with cassette tapes to add an audio dimension to the equipment. This occurs mostly in standardized, off-the-shelf programs provided by outside vendors. When the synchronization works, it has quite a magical effect. The slide moves effortlessly with the comments of the narrator or with the dramatization. When the synchronization does not work, the seminar leader has to substitute hand control and risk loosing synchronization with the sound track.

Easel Pad/Chalk Board. No seminar leader can function without a large-size pad mounted on an easel, or a chalk board. Either has many uses. For one thing, you can use it to record the responses of team leaders to an application exercise. Writing down responses makes them available for continuing reference. And it gives the other teams a chance to reflect on the answer given and compare it to their own. Putting it on the easel pad adds emphasis. Then too, you can make a continuing display of the points written by tearing off pages and taping them on the wall. Sometimes it is useful to flip back some pages in the pad and make a cross reference to a point made previously. Comparisons or relationships can sometimes more easily be explained through diagrams on the easel pad. Because of its great versatility, the easel pad seems to have largely replaced the blackboard and, to a lesser degree, the chalk board—both of which must continuously be erased and thus cannot "store" information for later reference.

Sound and Motion. Visuals with sound and movement used to be the province of 16mm motion pictures. Now, videotape or video disc equipment is rapidly coming to the fore. Projection-beam, large-screen capability for the video equipment will be an early development. All of the sound and motion vehicles offer imaginative opportunities for folding back the doors of the classroom. Dramatizations with high viewer appeal can be used to demonstrate how to do something or can be used as a basis for evaluation by the class as to how well something was done. The original production cost is high, but there are libraries of packaged video cassette and 16mm film material available to training directors through outside vendors.

One of the more important technological changes that has come into the seminar scene is the use of videotape equipment to tape and play back. The equipment has no equal in providing self evaluation or group critique of role plays. However, the initial investment in equipment is a significant capital expense, though it probably will become less so. Moreover, with present technology the screens are relatively small and require expensive multiplication of equipment.

Rear-View Projection. Almost all of the image projection equipment can be used in combination with rear-view projection facilities and equipment. That is, they can be placed in a soundproofed room behind the screen, and not be in the seminar room at all. The exceptions are the overhead projector, which has to be directly operated by the presenter, and video images, which (under current technology) are not really "projected," but created on the equipment's own screen. The rear-view technique effectively eliminates any problem of sound or any need to lower the room lighting. But it is expensive, has space requirements, and involves remote control equipment. Furthermore, if something goes wrong, the seminar leader is not in control.

Display Boards. Display boards can be used effectively in conjunction with other audio/visual techniques if there is some ongoing visualization that has a continuing usefulness for some significant portion of the seminar. For example, in one of our workshops on action planning, the story of one George Allison, who is undertaking a comprehensive product line study for his boss, is unfolded step-by-step. It proves quite useful to have a large organization chart of the company on each wall of the room as a continuing reference as to functions and people.

CRT Screens. Already widely used in programmed instruction for individuals, cathode ray tube visualizations are beginning to be used in various forms of computer-assisted instruction adaptable to seminars. Games played by teams in competition with each other offer exciting possibilities for intense participant interest combined with learning through application.

Planning the Visuals

It would be a rare training seminar today that would not be accompanied by visual aids planned and designed as an integral part of the seminar itself. Seminar leaders will introduce further visual aids during the seminar as appropriate, mostly via the easel pad, but possibly using blank acetate sheets and the overhead projector. These supplementary visuals will add to the impact of the program, but a standard set should be part of the seminar design process. In off-the-shelf programs provided by outside firms, a much greater use of visuals, coupled with a recorded narrator, may be used to facilitate the use of the program by many leaders with large participant populations. This is a way of ensuring that essentially the same message will be given to all participants.

When to Use. Visual aids provide visualizations to reinforce learning and should be used only when that purpose can be served. They should *add* visual interest or impact and accent a change of pace. One way they do this is by demonstrating relationships that are not easily made clearly understandable through words alone. There are many familiar examples of this. An organization chart is one. It quickly shows a structure of reporting relationships that cannot as easily be described in words. A visualization can present the relationships at a single glance. Other examples are flow charts, models, graphs, bar charts, and pie charts.

Another important use of visuals is for emphasis of important ideas. Participants not only hear an idea from the seminar leader, or read about it in a text, but they get reinforcement visually. The reinforcement can be quick, for example a slide summarizing key points. Or it may be more extensive, for instance a demonstration of an employee selection interview or a performance counseling session. Dramatizations such as these, which add human interest of real people, in action situations, can be thrown on the screen before the group.

Visuals can be used to clarify the structure of the presentation. "In this afternoon's session, we shall be covering seven guidelines to more effective communication," the presenter might say. Visuals listing the seven points and underscoring the point about to be made will then provide both orientation and reinforcement. However, each of the seven guidelines should be condensed as much as possible—to a single word or a brief phrase.

Visual aids can also be effectively used to provide a change of pace or method in order to maintain participant interest level. Too much lecture, too patterned a use of group discussion or team exercises, too much packaging, or cookie cutter similarity in anything can result in loss of participant interest. But visuals, skillfully used, can counter this problem—particularly if there are variations in projection technique and visual treatment. They have to be skillfully used because too much *sameness* in the use of visuals can add to monotony instead of providing high-interest, changes of pace.

How to Use Visual Aids. Skill in using visual aids can be a book or a course in itself, but there are a few highlights I can suggest from my experience:

1. *More Visualizations, Less Text.* The unique benefit of visual aids is to get quick understanding of ideas that cannot as easily be described in a sequence of words. In designing slides, therefore, we have to seek ways of exploiting this unique advantage. "A picture is worth a thousand words," the old saying goes, so let's use visuals to get this benefit.

2. *Keep Aids Simple and Concise.* In order to get the right impact, the visual should get the basic idea over quickly and simply. If text is used, it should be reduced to short, meaningful phrases. Let the seminar leader expand on each point as necessary or appropriate.

3. *Make Aids Legible.* Make sure the visuals can be read by all participants, including those in the rear of the room and those with less than 20/20 vision. If you are using text and have made the text simple and concise, you should be able to make the letters large enough to be easily read. By the way, experience suggests that upper and lower case is more easily read than solid capital letters.

4. *Make Each Visual Count.* Since emphasis is one of the important benefits achieved through visuals, you have to be selective. If you include everything, there *is* no emphasis. If something can be adequately covered in the workbook or orally, don't have a slide on it. This argues against the use of visuals for titles, definitions, or other subjects that can better be presented in the text, unless certain selected points need to be given special emphasis.

5. *Provide Variety.* Again, since one of the purposes of aids is to avoid monotony, you need to do that in the visuals themselves. Provide photographs of people and places mixed with flow dia-

grams, cartoons, and charts. For aesthetic reasons, you may want to use a common background color for text slides and a consistent lettering treatment. The principal danger here is an unvarying series of text slides. If practicable, alternate still image projections with moving ones, via videotape or motion pictures.

Seminar design does not stop with the initial program development; it continues, to a degree, as the seminars are being conducted, particularly with the visual aids. Some of these design changes may be formalized in new or revised visuals, new or revised handouts, or changes in the workbooks. But many of them will be trial-and-error improvizations by the seminar leader who is on the firing line, who has the final opportunity to make the adjustments needed for greatest success for each individual participant group. But even though some of the design will be a continuing process, it is the creative work done before the first pilot session that primarily determines the success of the program.

Chapter 7

Choosing the Seminar Setting

The best designed seminar may nevertheless fail if the seminar setting is wrong. Decisions involving the seminar room and layout are the most important; but the geographic location and supporting services and facilities have to be considered as well. Here are some ideas that may help in making those decisions.

IMPORTANCE OF THE SETTING

A good environment can't assure success, but a poor one can mean failure. If the participants can't see well, can't hear well, or are physically uncomfortable, they are not going to be able to learn very much. The same result comes about if the total setting is psychologically depressing or if there are distractions. Here are a few case examples in point.

One company, headquartered in Massachusetts, selected a religious retreat for a seminar setting. You might think that the overall spirit of peace, quiet, and spiritual dedication might be a plus; but you would be wrong. The sleeping rooms were small and bare, like cells in a medieval monastery. There was barely room for one straight back chair and one dresser in the floor area not taken up by the bed. The walls were painted an off-white, toward-tan color and had nothing on them—not even a religious picture or psalm. The only place for evening team sessions was the large, main reception lounge, which worked acceptably well the first night—each team congregating in a different location in the room. But on the two succeeding evenings, the lounge was overcrowded with noisy people who were gathering for a religious service. There was a brief respite during the service, but afterward they were all in the lounge again chattering happily with each other. The noise level was intensified by echoes from the uncarpeted floor and bare walls. Here and there, hardly observable within this milling mass of people, a participant team could be seen huddled together trying to discuss a Universal Products Company case.

On another occasion, because of airplane connection problems, a seminar leader arrived late for a meeting scheduled to start at 9:00 A.M. in the Hilton Hotel at O'Hare Airport in Chicago. She arrived to find twenty large individuals seated classroom style in a room that was no larger than a standard guest room with beds removed. It seemed to her that the oxygen in the air was close to being completely exhausted, replaced by the carbon dioxide emanating from all those lungs in a small room with low ceiling. The client coordinator had brought an overhead projector and screen; but because of the small size of the room they had to be so closely positioned to each other that the projected image seemed no larger than an 8½ x 11″ sheet of paper. Fortunately, the hotel was able to provide a substitute room, but a half day of the seminar was lost and many snide comments were made when the seminar leader got to the subject of "planning."

Another example involves a quite attractive suburban motor inn located on a fairly large piece of land, mostly parking lots, situated amid a complex of super-highways. The problem was that the "joggers" in the group—and there always seems to be a surprisingly large number of them—had no place to run in the early mornings. What space they could find was polluted by the fumes of closely speeding motor vehicles. Part of the purpose of running, I am told, is to wash out the lungs with repeated drafts of clean fresh air—a purpose defeated by this setting.

A final illustration took place in a new, luxurious, downtown hotel in New York City. Being new, the hotel staff was still getting its act in order. At exactly 4:00 on the next-to-last afternoon of the seminar, the door was supposed to open and the waiter roll in a table with cheese, wine, and fruit. The importance of timing had been stressed so fully upon the hotel staff that the seminar leader came carefully to a dramatic conclusion at 4:00 P.M., confidently expecting the seminar room door to open and the surprise feast to be rolled in; but nothing happened. He carried on as well as he could for five to eight minutes after this carefully planned climax had been reached, but finally had to go running out into the hall to see what had happened. The problem, as it turned out, was that the supplies had been delivered to the wrong seminar room! The participants were good sports about it; but the intended effect was completely lost.

GEOGRAPHIC OPTIONS

Geographic location is the question that is presented first in planning the seminar setting. Though geography may not be as important as the seminar room itself, you have to make decisions on overall location, as a rule, before you can establish and evaluate available alternatives on the seminar room and supporting services. Choosing the geographic location for the seminar may end up as a matter of personal preference, but there are some factors to consider. If the company has its own training facility, then the first question is whether or not to use it. If there is no company facility, or it is decided not to use it, the next practical question is whether you can find a suitable facility in your area of geographic preference for the dates you have set up for the seminar. Convenience to public transportation and cost are other factors to be considered. Here is a run down of the various alternatives with the advantages and disadvantages of each (see Figure 8).

Figure 8
COMPARISON OF DIFFERENT SEMINAR FACILITIES

Facility	Cost	Service	Access	Overall
Company conference center	No out-of-pocket cost	Good, but not lavish	Good	If you have one, use it
Company conference room	No out-of-pocket cost	Full services not required; breaks only	Excellent	Least costly, but potential too great for distractions and interruptions
In-town hotel	Expensive	Good	Excellent	Quite acceptable, if affordable
Conference center	Expensive	Excellent	Good	Ideal, if affordable

Figure 8 (*Continued*)
COMPARISON OF DIFFERENT SEMINAR FACILITIES

Facility	Cost	Service	Access	Overall
Suburban motor inn	Fairly expensive	Good	Good to excellent	Quite acceptable, more easily affordable
Remote retreat	Usually reasonable	Fair	Usually not too easily accessible	Varies

Company Conference Rooms

A company's own multi-purpose conference room in the organization's place of business has no equal in terms of low cost and convenience. Participants' commuting habits don't have to be changed. Transportation and sleep-away cost are avoided. The seminar leader and the participants may well be quite familiar with the setting and feel comfortable in it. It has many advantages.

Counterbalancing the cost advantage, however, are many disadvantages to the use of an organization's own conference room. For one thing, some of the participants will have their regular offices nearby, which serves as a continuing distraction. They may try to continue carrying on their jobs while attending the seminar, instead of committing themselves 100% to the training experience. They will not only be late for the morning and afternoon sessions and late coming back from breaks, they may miss whole periods of time because of some real or perceived emergency that keeps them in their offices. It is not always the fault of the participants themselves. Sometimes it is a problem caused by subordinates or superiors who put demands on the time of the participants.

Company Training Centers

Seminars held in company training centers located away from operating activities largely eliminate these disadvantages and introduce some further benefits. Because the superiors and subordinates of the participants are aware that they are not easily reached, interruptions are far less likely. At the same time, the participants are psychologically removed from their place of work. Day-to-day operating problems seem remote to them. Furthermore, the centers typically provide sleeping accommodations, which makes it possible for the seminar leader to make better use of evening assignments, particularly team exercises. There is a greater sense of comraderie, and the commitment of the participants tends to be intensified by the greater opportunity they have to interact with each other.

On the other hand, company training centers have disadvantages. If the training center is too comfortable, it can induce a "rest and recreation" attitude in the participants. If it is too Spartan, employees may not be eager to go there.

In-Town Hotels

Generally, the in-town hotel offers important advantages: easy transportation, attractive facilities, and good supporting services, although the extent of these advantages will differ from city to city and town to town. In major metropolitan centers like New York City, the cost can be very high, particularly for those who require sleeping accommodations. If you are only scheduling one or two seminars, you do not represent especially attractive business for the larger, more prominent hotels, and as a result you may not get the service that you would like. Depending on the city, there may also be some enticing evening distractions.

Conference Centers

Establishments that cater especially to companies conducting training sessions for their employees have sprung up in the past ten years or so. These conference centers understandably pay a great deal of attention to creating a favorable seminar environment. The meeting rooms are typically well sound-proofed. The chairs provided are more comfortable—they don't have to be "stacked" for storage, as in a hotel which has multiple uses for its conference rooms. Lighting controls are provided that permit finer adjustment to the differing needs of different types of projection equipment. Temperature/ventilation controls are easily accessible to the seminar leader. The total ambience, interior decor, and landscaping is likely to be attractive but not distracting.

By way of example, in the East there are the Harrison Conference Centers in Glen Cove, New York, and Southbury, Connecticut; the Tarrytown Conference Center in Tarrytown, New York; the Hilton Conference Center in Hightstown, New Jersey; the Sterling Forest Conference Center near Suffern, New York, and many others. In other parts of the country there are the Southern Conference Center, in Atlanta, Georgia; the Lanier Conference Center, Atlanta, Georgia; and the Woodlands Conference Center, in Houston, Texas, to name only a few.

Suburban Motor Inns

The suburban motor inn has become a very popular location for holding training seminars. There is usually a fairly large selection to choose from in any geographic area, and all of them will feature easy transportation to the nearby airport. Generally, they offer attractive facilities and good supporting services. They tend to be less expensive than the in-town hotel and more interested in seminar business.

But suburban motor inns have their disadvantages as well. Their seminar rooms have to serve multiple purposes: receptions, cocktail parties, or hospitality suites. As a result, there may be movable partitions for walls, which are not very soundproof. Chairs may be designed for easy stacking, rather than comfortable sitting. Lighting may be more appropriate for a social setting than for a seminar, and very likely will not be easily controllable by the seminar leader. There is a possibility that the room may have to be used in the evening for another function, which means that the participants cannot leave things in the room, nameplates will be disorganized, and the room will not be set up properly on the next day.

Interestingly enough, the suburbs are not free from enticing evening distractions. Almost without exception, a "rock" ensemble, with full frequency amplification, will play from 9:00 P.M. to 1:00 or 2:00 A.M. Many of these suburban motor inns have become active social centers for the surrounding areas.

Remote Retreats

Some companies go to unusual lengths to get their people away from civilization. The "remote retreat" offers the least possibility for interruption and the greatest opportunity for mutual commitment and challenging evening assignments, unless it is also a resort area or offers a too enticing variety of athletic and recreational facilities. One of our good clients features a motel in a remote location along the ocean in New Jersey. The motel looks right out over the ocean, but offers nothing by way of exercise or entertainment. Walkers or joggers can find an outlet for their energies—as can those who enjoy their fellowship at the bar. As long as the participants have interesting and demanding evening assignments it works well. If not, some enterprising soul will organize evening visits to the gaming tables in Atlantic City, an hour and a half drive away.

Charming as some of them may be, these remote retreats can present other problems. Transportation can be difficult. As a result, time away from the job can be increased by one or more days, simply in getting to and from the seminar site. Furthermore, there is some risk in the quality of supporting services, which will vary with the particular facility chosen. But if it is truly "remote," there is a strong likelihood of limited menus, no valet service, few telephones, and certainly no room service.

Resorts

In season, the use of vacation resorts for training seminars is probably out of the question because of the cost involved. For very special occasions, involving top management groups, it may be possible to use resorts. If so, it is virtually mandatory to provide some time off to use the golf course, tennis courts, and other facilities provided, for at least a portion of one day.

In the off season, the resort areas are more frequently used because favorable rates can be negotiated. It is difficult to generalize on these resort areas, since they all have their own unique characteristics. If you find one that suits your needs and is reasonably accessible, use it. You will find that many of these resorts are eager to develop off-season revenue and will treat you well.

THE SEMINAR ROOM

Selection of the seminar room is far more important to the success of the seminar than the geographic location and type of facility. The room in which the actual training will take place has to meet the physical and psychological needs of the participants and of the leader. In a very real sense, these needs resemble Frederick Herzberg's maintenance or hygiene needs with respect to motivation. If not met, these needs can have a negative influence. But they do not have a significantly positive impact. Similarly, meeting the participants' physical needs probably won't contribute much to the learning process, but it can most certainly prevent distractions that could detract from the success of the seminar.

Physical Considerations

The very real physical needs of participants have to be kept in mind in selecting the seminar room. Their minds cannot function with full effectiveness if their bodies are uncomfortable, as for example if they are too warm, if they are breathing stale air, if they are seated too close together, or if they are seated in uncomfortable chairs. Then again, they cannot learn at all if they cannot hear or see what is going on.

Temperature. Every experienced seminar leader knows the importance of being able to control the temperature. As the thermometer rises above 72°, there is an increase in lethargy and drowsiness and a decrease in the quality of group discussion. Seminar leaders prefer the temperature to be slightly on the cool side. But please don't go below 66°—or you again begin to lose the group. All of this underlines the importance of having a room in which the seminar leader can measure and control the temperature. Remember, though, in regulating temperature, that it is easy to go from one extreme to the other. If the room gets uncomfortably warm, the tendency is to push the temperature control sharply toward cooler and to forget it—until it gets uncomfortably cool. This tendency to go to extremes is one reason that many facilities make the control accessible only to their own engineers.

Ventilation. Closely related to temperature is the need for circulating air. If the proportion of carbon dioxide or cigarette smoke goes up, the concentration and involvement of the participants tend to go down. The need for fresh air would favor larger rooms, higher ceilings, and, again, means for the seminar leader to control circulation—even if by so simple a means as being able to open windows. Fortunately, ventilation is not usually a major problem in most modern facilities.

Vision. Lighting and room size should be such that everyone can easily see the instructor, projected visual aids, easel pad or chalk board, participant materials, and each other. Lighting controls should be conveniently located near the seminar leader's table, especially if the lights need to be dimmed to accommodate projection equipment being used. Sometimes you have to unscrew light bulbs that shine directly on the projection screen, to avoid turning down the lights during a visual presentation. If the ceiling isn't too high, the seminar leader can do this by standing on a chair. Otherwise, it takes a maintenance worker with a ladder, who always seems strangely resistant to unscrewing the bulbs—particularly fluorescent bulbs.

Hearing. Making sure that everyone can hear what's going on is usually not so much a problem with accoustics as it is a problem with interference. Should a loud 16mm sound movie go on in an adjoining room, it can be quite unsettling, both for the leader and the group. Though innkeepers stoutly maintain otherwise, the so-called movable partitions that are used to subdivide a large ballroom into separate salons do not provide ample protection against noise—at least this has been my experience.

Unfortunately, noise interference is not always avoidable through careful planning. At about 9:00 one morning, a crew with pneumatic drills attacked a sidewalk in need of repair directly under a second floor seminar room at the Nassau Inn in Princeton, New Jersey. The noise was deafening, although intermittent. The arrival of these workmen was something that could not have been anticipated when the facility was booked, six months prior. Although the incident became a subject of good-humored remarks, it nevertheless interfered with the learning process.

Sitting Comfort. There are three different aspects to the problem of sitting comfort and they are all important, especially since most seminar participants are unaccustomed to long periods of sitting in a classroom situation. The first is elbow room. Crowding people too closely together is to be avoided. Each person needs at least 2½, preferably 3 feet of space at the table. The second is knee room. In setting up the room, try to avoid having people sit right up against table legs. The third is comfortable chairs, upholstered if possible, with springs, or at least a soft cushion to sit on.

Sometimes, in spite of comfortable chairs, we encounter people with a physical problem that makes sitting for too long actually painful. This was explained to me once by the chairman of the board of a large, new client, who had a bad leg. Every so often, with an engaging smile, he would stand up for 5 or 10 minutes at his place. Even though we all understood the reason behind it, it always came as a bit of a surprise. The first few times, I thought he was getting up to make a point more forcibly. But no, that wasn't the case. He simply had to stretch his leg. Physical problems such as this one are not frequently encountered, but the story underlines the importance of physical comfort.

Psychological Considerations

Influences on the mental outlook of the group are almost as important as sheer physical comfort. The seminar room should be attractive and pleasing rather than discordant. And the whole setting should be free from distraction.

Decor. The overall color scheme and decoration plan can have an influence on the attitudes of the participants. But peoples' tastes will differ; you can't always please everybody. For this reason, you should avoid extremes of design and color. But don't bother to hire your own design expert. Your own judgment on what is reasonably attractive will be acceptable.

Space. Rooms that are too small or that have low ceilings can induce a feeling of psychological imprisonment in some people. You are better off if you err on the side of spaciousness and higher ceilings. More space in the room also has the practical benefit of facilitating break-away sub-group meetings without the need for separate break-away rooms. I can only recall one time that a seminar room was actually too large. It was a huge ballroom. Even at that, it worked reasonably well. The "U" shaped table was put at one end of the room and a number of circular tables for break-away sub-group meetings at the other end.

Layout. The layout of the seminar room has a direct effect on the amount and quality of interaction among the participants. The effect will be positive if the participants can all see each others' faces and nameplates. The way that you arrange the tables, chairs, and equipment to accomplish this interface depends upon the number of people in the seminar. For groups of seven or fewer participants, a conference type arrangement is to be preferred. A circular, oval, or rectangular table is used, with the seminar leader seated at one end of the table. For seminars with eight to twenty-five participants, the "U" shaped table is best, with the seminar leader at a small table at the open end of the "U" (see Figure 9). For larger groups, there are two options: grouping participants at a number of round tables or lining them up in rows, classroom style. If the seminar design calls for frequent sub-group exercises, the former would be more appropriate.

The rationale behind the equipment layout is to create a better learning environment, for which there are few absolute rules. The seminar leader has to position projectors, easels, and screens in a way that best suits the requirements of the seminar, the room, and his or her personal preferences. Overhead projectors can usually be placed on the leader's table or on a lower table alongside the leader's table. The projection screen, with a keystone remover attachment, should be placed behind the seminar leader, to one side and at an angle— positioned to produce a large enough projected image from the overhead projector. The placement of the overhead projector and screen in this way will prevent the seminar leader from obstructing the participants' view of the projected image on the screen.

Figure 9
PREFERRED SETUP FOR A 20 PARTICIPANT SEMINAR

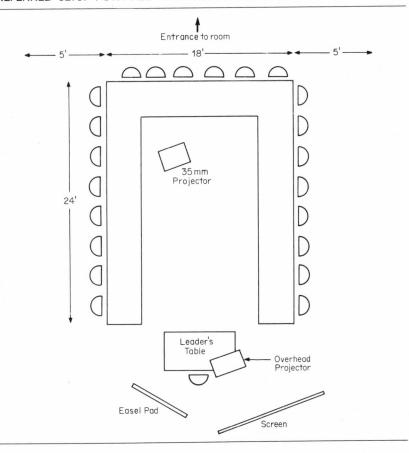

35mm projectors will have to be positioned twenty or thirty feet from the screen, either on a low table within the "U" or on a high stand behind a row of participants. The stand must be high enough to prevent participants' heads from casting shadows on the screen. In either case, an extension to the control cable is required. If the screen for the overhead projector has been tipped forward by means of a keystone correction attachment, you may need a second screen for the 35mm projector.

As to other equipment, lecterns should be avoided: they encourage lecturing and giving too much attention to notes. The easel pad should be positioned in accordance with the seminar leader's hand dominance. A right-handed leader will want the pad on the left, and a left-handed leader will prefer it on the right.

Noise. Noise can be a mental distraction, as well as a barrier to hearing the seminar proceedings. One of our associates reports an experience in point. At 3:00 one afternoon of the seminar he was conducting, sounds of dance music arose from a ballroom below the seminar room. It was off-season in one of those remote resorts. The motor inn was holding a tea dance for the enjoyment of a large population of retired citizens. They were obviously having a great time; but some of the familiar dance tunes started a few participants' feet to tap and their minds to reminisce. The music wasn't loud enough to prevent the participants from hearing the seminar leader, but it was a mental distraction.

Visual Distractions. Visual distractions can also impact unfavorably on the seminar in many different ways. But all these ways have one common aspect: windows to see through to the outside world. An outstanding example I've heard about took place some years ago at a resort hotel on the isle of Capri. One whole wall of the seminar room was made of glass and looked out over a beautiful swimming pool complete with deck chairs and attractive plantings. It was in fact a pleasant and restful outlook for most of the first morning. But then, at about 11:00 A.M., a group of attractive young women descended on the pool in their bikinis! There was absolute chaos in the all-male, away-from-home seminar group.

THE REST OF THE FACILITY

If you have found the perfect seminar room, you can afford to be somewhat less demanding when it comes to the surrounding facilities and services. And yet, the overall atmosphere of a place, the attitude of its staff, the quality of the food served, the comfort of its sleeping accommodations, its scenic outlook, and the availability of physical exercise and recreation—all of these can play a part in making the seminar a pleasant experience. But the more you insist on top quality, the more it's going to cost.

Problems with a facility are more likely to occur if it is not a conference center or a well-established hotel chain, like Hyatt, Marriott, and others. Here is a check list of the problems you can face:

1. Slow meal service, making people late for class.
2. Break service, not on time.
3. Telephones ringing in the seminar room.
4. Not enough public telephones near the seminar room.

5. Inconveniently located rest rooms.

6. Sleeping rooms too near the rock music band in the bar.

7. Poor food—too limited a menu or just poor quality.

8. Insufficient physical exercise facilities: swimming pools, tennis courts, exercise room, jogging trails, scenic walks.

9. Insufficient recreation facilities: television, video games, gaming rooms.

10. Uncooperative staff.

11. Poor message service.

12. No credit cards accepted.

13. Educational materials shipped to the facility not delivered to the seminar room—or worse yet, lost.

Not all of these possible problems can be surely avoided, but many of them can. A personal visit to the facility is well worth the time and money. It is surprising how attractive a place can be made to look in brochures. A seminar room just the right size and shape may have a pillar in the middle of your "U." If possible, talk to others who have used the facility. (It is curious to realize how seldom this is done.)

Securing the right facility within the funds available is a challenge that involves geographical convenience, some degree of isolation from participants' ongoing responsibilities, pleasant surroundings that are relatively free from distractions, adequate supporting services and—above all—a seminar room that facilitates learning. The right mixture of all these can add to the probability of success. The wrong mixture can bring failure. In Figure 10, we have provided a checklist that can help establish a proper setting for your seminar.

Figure 10
SEMINAR FACILITY CHECKLIST

1. AVAILABILITY on seminar dates
2. COST
   a. Rooms for participants
   b. Meals
   c. Seminar room
3. TRANSPORTATION CONVENIENCE
   a. Public or own car
   b. If public,
      1) Convenience
      2) Frequency
      3) Cost

Figure 10 (*Continued*)

4. SEMINAR ROOM
    a. Size
    b. Appearance
    c. Lighting
    d. Decor
    e. Outlook
    f. Sound projecting
5. SUPPORTING SERVICES
    a. Food
    b. Sleeping accomodations
    c. Recreation
    d. Exercise facilities
    e. Public telephone
    f. Quality of service
6. OVERALL
    a. Scenic outlook
    b. General decor
    c. Cleanliness
    d. Experience in hosting seminars

Chapter 8

Getting the Most Out out of Your Seminar Leaders

An effective seminar leader is the next link in the chain of prerequisites for a successful training seminar. The best designed seminar given in an appropriate setting is nevertheless subject to this further variable: the knowledge, attitudes, and skill of the seminar leader. Whether you use members of your own staff, non-training department employees, or even consultants, you have to be very much concerned with selecting, training, and motivating them to continued peak performance. The emphasis among these three concerns will differ depending on the resource you are using. If you or someone on your staff will be the seminar leader, you will be less concerned about the material in this chapter on selecting seminar leaders: you've already gone through the selection process. Training and motivating will be of greatest importance when you are using non-training department employees on a part-time, special assignment. Qualified consultants should come ready-trained and in most cases properly motivated, since their professional careers depend on their continued excellence.

SELECTION

One way or another, selecting the right person as seminar leader is a necessary starting point. Some people can do a top calibre job, some are adequate, and some simply cannot conduct stimulating seminars. Presented in the first part of this chapter are some ideas to help you choose those who can put on a superior performance, whether they are candidates for positions as trainers in your department, non-training department employees, or consultants.

Importance

The importance of the seminar leader in putting on a successful seminar is second only to the seminar design. Anyone who has had experience in training people to conduct seminars will tell you that there can be a wide gap between the best and the least qualified of any group. I have had a great deal of experience teaching client personnel to conduct our off-the-shelf programs. It is a matter of great concern to me that I don't entrust our programs to leaders who lack the ability or desire to make them "sing."

To illustrate, I had to train two people from two different client organizations in one of our programs at the same time, not too long ago. Both were experienced in various personnel functions, including training. Both were attractive, articulate, and seemingly self-confident. But when I put them through some "dry runs" or practice presentations, it turned out they were worlds apart. One of the two enjoyed being "on stage." Her words came easily and clearly, her eyes confidently seeking out members of the make-believe audience. The other was unbelievably inept. He had trouble expressing his ideas, rambled, and let his eyes wander around the room and even focus on the ceiling! He could not be qualified as a trainer.

For another example, a newly appointed "training specialist" was clearly inadequate as a seminar leader. He had been transferred from a field sales job and was being trained in one of our programs as a first step in his new job. After discussing it with his boss, we all decided—including the training specialist—that we were fortunate to discover his inadequacies at the outset. It could have been a serious problem for this individual, and his career, if he had been allowed to continue in his new job and to become a highly visible failure.

Sometimes the problem is not one of ability, but of attitude. The problem occurs in two ways. One recurring problem is the disinclination of professional trainers to go through a leader's regular training program because it is "beneath" them. I know from sad experience that I have to insist on the training and see that they get enthusiastic about the program, or else not sell it to them. The other kind of problem is the lack of commitment on the part of a professional trainer who has not participated in the evaluation and selection of the program being conducted. I remember a recent example of this second situation. The training director involved inherited an off-the-shelf program purchased by her predecessor with some left-over budget money. Quite naturally, she viewed the program as someone else's program. She had no emotional involvement. If it doesn't go over, she will feel it is the fault of the program. She will not perceive it as her own lack of commitment.

Selection Criteria

What is important in choosing the right seminar leader? What criteria should be used in the selection process? Here are some ideas I have accumulated from personal experience and observation and discussion with others involved in conducting seminars.

Credibility. First of all, the seminar leader you put before trainee groups should be someone whose position, background, or personal impact predisposes these groups to accept the ideas presented. The outside consultant usually carries high credibility. In choosing from within, give preference to line managers and higher ranking people who tend to be given greater credence than others. The need for credibility is greater with higher-level participant groups, which probably explains the proportionately greater use of consultants at these levels as compared to lower-level groups.

Personal Effectiveness. The personal impact of the seminar leader is a second important criterion; it is closely related to credibility, but nevertheless has a somewhat different focus. Those who are generally perceived as "winners" or "comers" will tend to be more successful as seminar leaders. Those viewed as "misfits" or "losers" will be less successful. The presence and bearing of the individual is important here. Recently, a training director made an appropriate analogy to the television debates of Jimmy Carter and Ronald Reagan in 1980. Mr. Carter appeared worried and ill at ease. Helped no doubt by his professional background, Mr. Reagan projected an image of relaxed self-confidence, which surely must have been a factor in his successful campaign. The same kind of personal impact is important for seminar leaders.

Commitment. Look for people who have a high, positive motivation toward training. Serving as a seminar leader offers a great opportunity for self-development, which could appeal to people who are motivated to develop their own knowledge and skills. But don't get too carried away with this idea, as did one of the major commercial banks in

New York City. The bank deliberately selected, as instructor for each session of a multi-session management course, the officer that most needed improvement in that subject! Thus, the bank's poorest communicator ended up teaching "communication," and the poorest delegator, "delegation." It would appear that the objective of training the seminar leader may have been served at the expense of the participant groups.

Discussion Leadership Skills. The ultimate success of seminar leaders will depend mostly on their skill in drawing people out and in guiding intelligent and meaningful group discussions. Look for prior successful experiences in discussion leadership. If the person you're considering has no prior experience, here are some personal attributes that I have generally found in people who become effective discussion leaders; some of these can only be fully tested in the leader training process:

1. Oral communication facility.
2. Presence, in front of groups.
3. Sensitivity to people; being a good listener.
4. Adaptibility.
5. Native intelligence, quickness of mind.
6. Sense of humor.
7. Warmth of personality.

Knowledge of Subject Matter. Although not always essential, some degree of prior knowledge and experience in the subject matter of the seminar is certainly a "plus." Knowledge of the subject matter not only facilitates the leader training process, it gives the seminar leaders personal experiences and insights to share with participant groups, thus adding interest and credibility. If you are searching for someone to do management training, look for individuals with a minimum of ten years actual management experience. They will have greater credibility. There is an analogy here to some university professors whose lectures lack all the accepted hallmarks of effective oral communication, but whose knowledge of the subject matter is so vast as to hold large student classes spellbound.

TRAINING

Once the seminar leaders are selected, they have to be thoroughly trained to ensure the success of the seminar. The extent and intensity of this training will vary, depending on the subject matter and the pre-existing knowledge and skills of the leaders selected. The danger here is to assume too much. It is far better to err somewhat on the side of too much training, being sensitive on occasion to protecting the egos of those trainers who consider themselves already fully qualified.

Scope

The scope of leader training provided, at least to non-professionals, should include the following:

Subject Matter Content. Your seminar leaders should know the subject matter of the seminar so well that they exude confidence and can deal effectively with any questions that are presented to them in the seminar.

The Adult Learning Process. The discussion leaders you select should also be made to understand what is involved in the learning process so that they can properly fill their role. If they understand that the first step in the learning process is motivation, they are much more likely to stress the importance and relevance of each new subject as it comes along. If they truly understand the importance of testing, application, and feedback, they are far less likely to rely on pure lecture as a methodology. They will seek out contributions from the group and provide opportunities to demonstrate the quality of learning that is taking place.

The Seminar Design. It is of overriding importance that the seminar leaders become fully familiar with the seminar design. Only with a sound understanding of the basic design can your seminar leaders make sound adaptations to meet the needs of different participant groups. The "Leader's Guide" serves as the primary educational tool during leader training and a primary reference source later.

Discussion Leadership Techniques. Another vitally important subject to include in seminar leader training is discussion leadership techniques. Your future seminar leaders should learn how to use open questions and directed questions to initiate group discussion, how to encourage the sharing of relevant experiences, and how tactfully to control these discussion.

Administration and Logistics. Particularly important for non-training department, part-time seminar leaders is a complete orientation on administration and logistics. How are the participants selected? What is the schedule of seminars? How are schedule changes to be made? Who is in charge of securing the facility, room reservations, and equipment? What equipment is needed? How is it operated? What educational materials are to be provided to the participants? Who is responsible for making sure these materials are available? How do they deal with emergencies? What about certificates of completion? Seminar evaluation forms? Name plates? All relevant questions of this nature should be covered during the leader training session.

For example, as videotape equipment and course-ware come into more general use, seminar leaders have to be trained to use them. A significant portion of the training process may have to be concerned with the operation of the audio-visual equipment. In the middle 1970s, when a number of firms introduced packaged programs using cassette tapes synchronized with 35mm slides, equipment was a major problem. Only certain cassette tape players would interface properly with certain 35mm carousel projectors. If you didn't have the right marriage, or if you didn't operate the equipment properly, the slides wouldn't advance and the seminar leader would either have to advance them manually or not use them at all.

Method

The method to be used in training leaders will vary, depending on the type of seminar, the subject matter, and the number and pre-existing qualifications of the seminar leaders. The greatest care and attention will be required for new trainers or non-training department people on part-time assignment. To a greater or lesser extent, you have to consider the appropriate use of self-study, workshops, self-evaluation, auditing others, and learning by doing.

Self-Study. Learning comes from within. People can be helped to learn in many useful ways; but it is really up to them. Self-study or self-development, using materials that you can provide, has to be a primary means of training your seminar leaders. The larger the population to be trained, the more care and attention you have to pay to providing the materials they need for self-teaching.

Workshops. Group sessions with practice presentations and critiques represent another method, a pre-requisite where groups of people are being trained. Practice presentations with videotaping and play-back and group critiques take up the major portion of these workshops. The critiques have to be managed carefully so as to build and not weaken the participants' self-confidence. Good points have to be stressed. Only a few—the most important—opportunities for improvement should be identified in any single critique.

Learning by Example. In training new members of our own staff, I have found over the years that they can learn a great deal by auditing experienced professionals. Your seminar leaders can do likewise. They can also learn by taking an active role in critiquing other trainees in the seminar leader workshop. But there is a small word of caution. In choosing "models" to copy, they should recognize that they have to establish their own styles. A good example is the use of humor. Some people have a great gift for knowing when a funny story would be appropriate and for delivering it with style. Others have trouble with jokes and should avoid them. A "punch line" that gets no laughs can detract from the rapport that is needed between leader and participants.

Learning by Doing. Developing skill as a seminar leader comes down to application or doing. Just as golfers develop skills on the practice tee or on the golf course, so seminar leaders become proficient by actually conducting the seminar. Practice presentations during the formal training period can simulate conducting the seminar, but the final skill development occurs most importantly during the first few presentations with live participant groups. The process is most effective if accompanied by qualified feedback, as it is in the leader training workshop.

MOTIVATING

Now that you have a trained seminar leader, how do you ensure his or her continued enthusiastic commitment? If you have a good seminar design, and established a favorable setting in which it will be delivered, you have enhanced the probability of success for your seminar leaders. Experiencing that success will in itself be a strong continuing source of motivation for them. If you have selected the right people, they will enjoy the ego-gratification provided by the esteem of successive seminar groups. Nevertheless, it is important to consider with some care the various motivational factors involved in keeping your seminar leaders properly motivated.

Growth and Development

The opportunity for growth and development is the first motivational factor to be considered. It is quite likely that the opportunity for self-development is what attracted people toward the assignment in the first place. The learning takes place in preparing and conducting the seminar. Every teacher will freely admit that learning is a two-way street. Every seminar provides a learning opportunity for the seminar leader as well as for the trainees. Sometimes this learning comes directly out of contributions made by participants. Sometimes the leader is forced to new depths of understanding by difficult questions that are posed, or by finding new ways to teach difficult ideas. The importance of the learning opportunity as a motivational influence on the leader is undoubtedly greater in the earlier stages of the program than it is in the later stages, but is nevertheless of continuing importance.

Ego Gratification

"I look for people who went out for dramatics in school and college," said one training director. "It's a clue that they really enjoy being 'on stage.' " The quote highlights the second motivational factor—ego gratification or the emotional need for experiencing the favorable response of others. The analogy to dramatics is a good one. Enthusiasts of the live stage talk about the magic rapport that builds between players and audience. The favorable response of the audience acts as an emotional stimulant to the actor or actress. Even though the same lines may have been given hundreds of times before, there is a new freshness, a new spontaneity that comes directly from the action and reaction that takes place across the footlights.

Some of the best seminar leaders I know have ego needs that must be continuously fed by the appreciation and applause of participant groups. These leaders will tell you that the same electric rapport that develops between dramatic actors and audience in the theater also develops between trainer and trainees in a seminar. These presenters sometimes make a game of it—to see how long it takes them to "win over" each participant group.

Achievement

A third motivational factor, a sense of achievement, is also present in a seminar setting. Some of it is intangible, coming out of a realization that the trainees are in fact learning. Some of it comes verbally from the participants themselves, either directly to the leader during the course of the program or in written evaluations at its close.

Professional trainers also find a sense of achievement in testing and making modifications in the way they present certain subjects. So long as these variations do not affect the integrity of the seminar, they should be encouraged and given adequate recognition. Sometimes the modifications can be built back into the seminar leader's guide or communicated to other leaders of the same seminar. The process of continuing modification also acts as a hedge against boredom, although this is not as much of a problem as is commonly believed. Hardly a seminar goes by that is conducted by our firm without some participant asking the presenter, "How many times a year do you give this program?" It seems difficult for them to realize that each group is different, made up of different personalities interacting and reacting in different ways. Group discussions take new twists, new questions are asked, and minor modifications are always being tested out by the presenter.

Recognition

The first three motivational factors discussed above are essentially established by the seminar setting; but this one—recognition—is more directly under the training director's control. Therefore, it may be the most important. By recognition, we mean more than the response of the participant group, although that is also important. Rather, we are referring to the type of recognition that a training director or the company management can provide.

One of our associates had a positive experience that illustrates this point. He has for some years conducted a specially designed management course for higher-level managers in a prominent publishing company. It had become customary for the president of the company to join the group one night during the week for cocktails and dinner. On this particular occasion our associate was unable to attend the function. However, he learned afterward that the president had singled him out, by name, for some very complimentary remarks during the course of the evening.

The example suggests one way of providing recognition. But there are others. Special mention can be made in newsletters or in the company's internal publication. Awards can be given and certificates awarded. A letter of appreciation from the senior vice president, human relations—or from the president—can sometimes be used with good effect. But as in other aspects of motivation, these measures have to be sincere and in response to demonstrated accomplishment.

This type of recognition can go a long way in maintaining high motivation in seminar leaders. But the other motivational factors—growth and development, ego gratification, and a sense of achievement—are very much dependent on selecting the right people to present the seminars and giving them the training that will ensure success.

Chapter 9

Managing the Seminar

Up to now, you have been concerned with all the things that have to take place in advance of the seminar. In this chapter and the next, you are on the firing line. You have come in this narrative to the seminar itself. You need to consider all the things that have to go right during the conduct of the seminar to give it maximum effectiveness. The focal point now shifts from the training director to the seminar leader, who may in some cases be the same person. Here is the payoff. If everything has been done right to this point, the odds greatly favor success. But the odds say not everything has gone right, which provides a continuing challenge to seminar leaders. In addition, they have to manage groups of fifteen to twenty-five participants who themselves represent different mixtures of experience, personalities, and motivation.

The management role of seminar leaders in conducting the seminar can easily be overlooked. Their role as a communicator, covered in the next chapter, is more dramatic and more visible. But nevertheless, they are managers—managers of the seminar. They have to *plan* the progress of the seminar. They have to *organize* the participants into sub-groups or teams, and *delegate* work to them. They have to oversee the provision of supporting services. And they have to provide ongoing *control.*

PLANNING

Most of the planning has already been done when the seminar leaders arrive at the seminar site to conduct the program. But nevertheless, you have to make a last-minute check on the execution of the plan to determine if any last-minute improvisation is necessary. The set-up of the seminar room—tables, chairs, equipment, and educational materials—is seldom just right. Fine-tune adjustments often have to be made to the schedule and subject matter to meet the special requirements of the particular participant group. Unless you do these things, you may have to suffer with a poor room layout; you may lack needed educational materials when it comes time to use them; and you most surely will run out of time or run out of things to say or do during the time available.

Double Checking Arrangements

Seminar leaders who fail to check out all the seminar arrangements before starting the seminar quickly learn better. No matter how reliable the administrative backup, there are always problems. Hopefully the mistakes are little ones: too many or too few chairs, no speaker's table, or perhaps the open end of the "U" is facing the wrong way. But sometimes more serious problems are presented: no workbooks, no projector, or a burned-out bulb with no available spare; and corrective measures have to be promptly instituted.

Ideally, you should check everything the night before the seminar begins. It may be difficult to fight your way through well-intentioned but unresourceful employees, but most facilities will have an assistant manager, maintenance worker, or engineering department representative hidden around somewhere. If you persist, you can find one of them. If you can see to everything the night before, you'll sleep better.

Even if the set-up crew has done a good job, there are important preliminaries that are usually beyond its capabilities. Educational materials have to be distributed to be ready for the participants when they arrive. The screen, projectors, and flip-charts have to be carefully positioned. Your visuals have to be mounted in carousels or placed in proper sequence.

Ideally you should have everything in place by the time the partici-pants come in. It is always a little disconcerting when early arrivals find you rushing around to put things in order. I usually put the early birds to work distributing educational materials and they are always happy to do so.

A useful planning tool in providing yourself with last-minute reas-surance is a seminar checklist. You'll want to make your own, but to give you some ideas we have provided you with the checklist that we use in Figure 11.

Figure 11
SEMINAR CHECK LIST

THE ROOM
   Lighting
   Ventilation
   Temperature
THE LAYOUT
   Number of places set
   Configuration
   Space for leader
   Leader's table and chair
THE MATERIALS
   Workbooks
   Acetate sheets
   Felt pens
   Leader's biography
   Handouts
   Rosters
   Name cards or plates
   Pads
   Pencils
   Projection equipment
      type and number
      functioning
      placement
      spare bulbs
      extension cord wires taped down
   Easels
   Chalkboard
   Easel pads
   Chalk or markers
   Pointer
   Charts, maps, exhibits

Figure 11 (*Continued*)

SUPPORTING SERVICES
  Time schedule for breaks
  Location
  Menu

Accommodating To Participants' Backgrounds

The more you can learn in advance about the group that will form the seminar, the better prepared you can be. You'll need to know their general level of knowledge and experience in order to set your pace and difficulty level. How will this group relate to some of your favorite stories and examples? How can you rework them to be more appropriate?

One example comes to mind from an early point in my own presenting career. I had to substitute, on fairly short notice, for another seminar leader in presenting a seminar on professional management to a group of higher-level executives in a large retailing company. Although I was still somewhat of a novice, I thought it went reasonably well. However, I learned later from my associate that the group thought the examples I used were drawn too heavily from my own previous experience. I had not reworked them to become more relevant to retailing executives.

Sometimes you even have to watch your language mannerisms. Some years ago the American Tobacco Company was pushing the slogan "Lucky Strike Extra," which crept into my own everyday vocabulary to mean providing something more than might be expected. I didn't realize how much a part of my language habits the phrase had become until I caught myself about to use the phrase in a seminar with executives from R. J. Reynolds Industries!

Planning Daily Schedules

Another important aspect of seminar leader planning is pace or timing. You have to think through the timing of the material to be covered during the day. No matter how well-defined the time schedule might be in the seminar design, presenters have to adjust the schedule to each participant group and to local conditions. Starting or finishing times may be set for the seminar that are different from those contemplated in the seminar leader's guide. Also, adaptations to provide for a faster pace or for more team exercises for particular groups have to be reflected in this adjusted time schedule.

One of the hallmarks of truly professional seminar presenters is to be able to arrive at each break and at the end of the day precisely on time and at natural stopping points. The way to do this is to put into your notes the time you plan to arrive at each separate subject in the seminar. Put the time in pencil so that you can easily change it for the next seminar. With the whole day scheduled in your notes, you'll find it easier to reschedule later sections if earlier ones run longer or shorter than planned.

You should also plan your options: material that can be used or omitted depending on the time available, or material that can be covered in alternate ways. Straight lecture takes the least time but is also the least interesting to participants. Group discussion will take somewhat longer but will not take as much time as team exercises. Seminar leaders in training worry most about having something useful to say to fill in the time available. But the problem is almost always the reverse: trimming back the material to fit the available time.

CONTROLLING

Your plan is useful only to the extent you keep checking your progress against it. Having planned the time to be devoted to each subject, you have to control the pace of the seminar against the plan and have to control the group to keep their discussions relevant and useful. Your control has to be exercised unobtrusively and with a reasonable degree of flexibility. You want to encourage free and easy participation. Constant interruptions and reminders that "we must be moving on now" will discourage participation and may develop frustrations.

Time Control

The rule for keeping a good control over time is simple: keep constantly aware of actual time as compared to plan. Place a watch face up on your table to which you can casually refer without anyone noticing it. The watch should have a face or numbers large enough to be read several paces away. A pocket calculator with stop watch and alarm beep capabilities can be helpful in timing team exercises; especially if you are visiting from team to team and are away from your table. Avoid using a wrist watch. There is no way to check the time unobtrusively. Looking at your wrist watch requires an arm-swinging motion that telegraphs to the class that there you go, checking the time again. It interrupts their concentration on subject matter.

There are a number of ways you can respond to a time overrun or shortfall. If you have allowed a discussion to continue beyond its allotted time, you'll need to foreshorten the time you use up on some subject coming up at a later point. If you have already planned some options to use, put them into effect. Otherwise you have to improvise. Team exercises can be foreshortened by eliminating questions or by assigning different questions to different teams instead of all questions to all teams. With fewer questions to consider, the teams will need less time to reach a consensus. Another emergency recourse is to speed up your treatment of less important subjects by referring participants to appropriate sections of the workbook and briefly summarizing them. As a general rule, though, try to foreshorten *your* portion of the seminar—not the participants' portion.

If you are running ahead of schedule, you are better off than if you are running behind. You can introduce optional work exercises or group discussions already planned for such an eventuality. Throw out some provocative questions to generate some group discussion and keep it going: "As you reflect on the subject we've just been discussing, where in your experience are managers most likely to go wrong?"

A final thought on controlling time is to start as well as end on time. Let the latecomers feel a slight embarrassment that the seminar has already begun. They'll quickly get the point. One seminar leader, who has a particularly good collection of funny stories, starts the afternoon session with one of his stories. If you're not back from lunch on time you may miss out on it! In rare cases, you may have to raise the question of timeliness during the session. Without making a threat of it, you can point out that starting late means finishing late because there is so much material to cover. A subtle tactic is to "synchronize watches" at the start of each day. Also, don't say, "please be back in 15 minutes," say, "please be back by 10:35."

Subject Matter Control

The other aspect of control concerns subject matter. Although you want to encourage free and full participation in group discussions, you nevertheless do have to keep the seminar moving. Group discussion that is allowed to continue for too long or go too far afield is not only a waste of valuable time, it will also annoy or bore some participants and weaken your leadership role.

Exactly how long to let a discussion continue is a matter of good judgment. You have to sense the extent and degree of group involvement. If you can see that every member of the group is keenly interested and the discussion is relevant, let it continue. Sooner or later you'll pick up some non-verbal clues that interest is waning, or perhaps the comments made will become obviously repetitious. Sometimes continuation of the discussion is being maintained by a single highly involved individual. In such cases it is time to step in. The group is ready to be rescued and move on. If you have the gift for cutting in with a humorous one-liner, by all means do it. Sometimes you can seize upon a comment of a participant as a natural bridge to the next subject. Calling a break is an easy way to terminate the discussion.

Controlling the subject matter of discussions also means making sure all the valid points are made. Leader's guides typically include "anticipated responses" to help the leader ask appropriate questions to draw these responses out of the group if they were not all forthcoming: "What arguments can you make on the other side of the case?" If necessary, fill in the missing ideas yourself.

Behavior Control

The problem of individual behavior comes up every once in a while. It appears in a variety of ways: the dominator who takes personal charge of every group discussion; the joker who is always out to get a laugh from the group; the wallflower who won't participate. One of the most disconcerting, I find, is the silent sphinx whose unchanging facial expression can be interpreted as hostility, detachment, or stupidity. You're never sure which. Once in a rare while, you run across active hostility.

In a surprisingly high proportion of the cases, the group itself will deal with the behavior problem. I can remember, early in my presenting career, a particularly troublesome individual. He was openly disrespectful to me and to other participants. He would inject inappropriate comments into group discussions. His behavior apparently was especially annoying to an older, huge-proportioned plant manager from Buffalo who happened to be sitting next to the offender at luncheon on the second day of the seminar. The plant manager, reacting to the problem participant's most recent remark, said, "You know what? You're something of a son of a bitch!" To my great surprise, the remark drew only a laugh, but from that point on, the problem disappeared.

In another instance, I had to deal with a persistently hostile and articulate fellow. It was a workshop in which the participants were being trained to develop objectives and standards of performance. He insisted repeatedly on raising the question of why anyone should need these things. He also stated quite positively that he could write up his own objectives and standards in half an hour without any need to go to a workshop. After trying to reason with him on these questions and calling upon others in the group to reason with him also, I finally said that if he didn't feel he needed the training, he was free to leave the seminar. After a moment's reflection, he got up and left—much to the collective relief of the whole group. Not to mention the seminar leader!

Behavior problems usually don't come up in such a forceful fashion and are not too difficult to handle. The discussion dominator can be deliberately passed over and questions fed to others in the group. Sometimes a quiet word with an overly talkative participant at the end of the day will help. Dozers and daydreamers can be roused by a direct question or by physically moving yourself directly in front of them for a few moments. Direct questions will also get the shy members of the group into the action.

At various times during the course of the seminar, you are called upon to take some action to keep the group under control. Fortunately, peer pressure is itself a powerful control on behavior problems. Use the other participants as necessary, but remember you have to keep control of the subject matter and the flow of proceedings against the established time schedule. Skilled seminar leaders have the capability of maintaining full control over the group while seeming to allow every opportunity for participation. They know exactly where they are in terms of the schedule, making departures to take advantage of the interests of the group. They never appear to be rushing even if in fact they are. This firm but relaxed control engenders the respect of the group and enhances the effectiveness of the seminar.

ORGANIZING THE PARTICIPANTS

Another management function exercised by seminar leaders is organizing the participants into sub-groups or teams and delegating projects to them. You assign participants to seat locations and in this way predetermine the composition of sub-groups that are established during the day by grouping nearby participants into teams. Decisions of this nature are more important in seminars of longer duration and those making greater use of team or sub-group exercises.

A rule of thumb that works well is to provide for constant change, primarily because it offers participants an opportunity to share their views and experience with more and different people over the course of the seminar. First, you can rearrange nameplates every evening to set up new members on the next day's teams. If you wish, you can make up rotation charts to ensure that each participant gets the greatest possible exposure to the other participants. Another way to provide for change is to make varying use of teams of two or three which can be formed in place. Teams of four or five will work better at "break-away" tables or in "break-away" rooms.

Increasingly these days, my simple rule is made more complex by the increasing assertiveness of non-smokers. It sometimes becomes necessary to form a kind of "leper colony" in one portion of the room for the smoking group. I still remember when I first encountered the problem, back in 1978. It was my first seminar with the prestigious Kraft, Inc. in Glenview, Illinois, at a high corporate level. "Gentlemen," our sponsor said to the group of mostly vice presidents assembled for the session, "we have made special arrangements for the convenience of the smokers: we'll have a fifteen-minute break in the middle of the morning, and another one in the mid-afternoon." When the significance of this sank in, I noticed there were no ashtrays on the conference table! The non-smokers had taken complete charge!

On occasion, seminar leaders have to be sensitive to individual physical problems. Those with poor vision or hearing should be seated toward the front. If some participant turns up one day with certain types of digestive problems, a seat near the door will be appreciated by all.

DELEGATING

Every time you break the group into separate teams you give assignments to the teams, which is a form of delegation. Sometimes you delegate a work assignment to individuals as well. In order for these assignments to be carried out effectively, there are a number of useful guidelines to follow.

Have a Clear Objective

Before sub-groups can function effectively, you have to have clearly in your mind what the end-result or objective is to be. Do you want them to evaluate how some character in a case study performed something? Or do you want to know how the participant team would have gone about doing it? Do you want them to outline the main points of their answer on an acetate? Or simply report orally? If you don't have these things clearly in mind at the outset, you cannot expect them to know what is required.

Consider the Capabilities of the Group

You also need to know your participants. You need to have a good idea that the assignment is difficult enough to challenge them but not so difficult as to be threatening. There are various ways that standard seminar case or exercise questions can be simplified or intensified based on your assessment of the participant group. For example, "What did Fred Nott do right and what did he do wrong?" is somewhat easier than, "Assume you are Fred Nott. Using all the material that we have covered on planning so far, explain step-by-step how *you* would have gone about developing a plan for Universal Products Company."

Make Sure They Have a Clear Understanding

The participants have to understand what it is you want them to do and, ideally, should have a real desire to do it. If they don't understand what has to be done, they can't do it. If they don't really want to do it, they'll do a slip-shod job. If you make a quick visit to each team shortly after the assignment is given, you can make sure there is no misunderstanding and can perhaps also shape more favorable attitudes. You'll find a much closer interpersonal relationship with your participants in these visits to the sub-groups than there is when the participants are all part of a single, large group discussion.

Establish and Keep Control

The last step in the delegating technique is to establish and keep control. It involves three primary considerations in the seminar setting. The first deals with timing. Make it clear at the outset how much time is allowed for the assignment. Then provide a "two-minute warning" before the time is up—an analogy to professional football which usually draws a smile, or perhaps a question on "how many time outs."

The second consideration is to appoint or get the sub-groups to elect team leaders. The mantle of team leadership should be spread among different participants to prevent strong personalities from excessive domination. In any event, the team leaders can exercise control within the sub-groups.

Finally, you have to be alert enough to step in and help weak teams to get back on the right track. You want each team to get some feeling of positive accomplishment and some recognition. You certainly don't want them to be embarrassed before their peers. For these reasons, you should provide appropriate help when you sense or perceive that it is necessary.

Whether it is in getting sub-groups to work effectively, in steering the discussion, in planning and controlling the progress of the seminar in time, or in ensuring the necessary support services from the seminar facility—in all these ways, seminar leaders function as the on-site managers of their seminars. This management role can be particularly demanding if there has been a breakdown in any of the steps leading up to the event. Seminar leaders need to be armed with names and telephone numbers of people to contact for any emergency problems. They need to exercise good judgment and flexibility in managing the participants and the seminar itself.

Chapter 10

Conducting the Seminar

The exciting challenge faced by seminar leaders at the start of each program is to communicate ideas and information in such a way as to create full understanding and enthusiastic acceptance. They have considerable help in doing so. The seminar design has already structured the subject matter in a sequence and schedule that should facilitate understanding. The seminar leader's guide provides a fairly precise course to follow. Educational materials and visual aids have been established to do the same thing. But seminar leaders have to put it all together. They also have to improvise from time to time and depart from the basic design. For both of these reasons it should be useful to start from some fundamentals and offer some observations on how seminar leaders can most effectively play their vital role as communicators.

There are seven guidelines that have been developed, to be considered in turn:

1. Know your seminar objective and subject matter.
2. Know your participants.
3. Get and keep them motivated.

4. Secure their understanding of the subject matter.
5. Ensure retention.
6. Get feedback.
7. Secure application.

KNOW YOUR SEMINAR

The first and critically important guideline is to know the seminar objective and subject matter. Keeping the objective in mind at all times is essential in determining relevance and priorities. Knowing your subject matter gives you confidence that you can deal expertly with any questions that come up. In a way, it's like playing golf. There are four stages of development: (1) unconscious incompetence, (2) conscious incompetence, (3) conscious competence and (4) unconscious competence. Complete beginners are *unconscious* of their *incompetence*. As they begin to play more golf they become *conscious* of their *incompetence* and may try to do something about it. If they do, they enter the next stage, which is *conscious competence*. They begin to know what they have to do and must concentrate on every aspect of the stance, grip, and swing to do it. The true professionals have so grooved their swings that they become *unconsciously competent*. They don't have to worry about fundamentals. They concentrate on tactics and the correct mental attitude. Likewise, when seminar leaders really know their subject, they become competent without the need to concentrate on what they are going to say next. It becomes second nature.

Knowing your subject gives you a great deal of self-confidence. You know you can probably answer any question the group throws at you. You are surer to be able to think up the right questions to lead group discussions. Your command of the subject matter will become quickly apparent to the group and greatly heighten your credibility.

Once, in auditing a seminar leader, I had a first-hand experience with the problems that develop if the subject matter knowledge is lacking. As the questions started coming to him, it became painfully obvious that he was groping ineffectually for the proper responses. It was almost as if the group knew they "had him on the ropes," the way they went after him. At one point, the struggling presenter had to turn to me for help, which further reduced his credibility with the group.

Perhaps a better example is Lou Allen, as described to me by the training director of a large and prominent company: "You know, Lou

Allen is not a very dynamic or forceful discussion leader. In fact, his voice sometimes drops down so softly that you can hardly hear him. But everyone leans forward with rapt attention because of his vast knowledge of professional management."

KNOW YOUR PARTICIPANTS

Knowing your participants ranks in importance with knowing your seminar. Here are the reasons why:

1. You can talk at the "right level." If you talk over their heads, they won't understand the ideas and information you are presenting. If you talk "down" to them, they'll resent it and lose interest in the seminar.

2. You are better able to call on the right people to add meaning to a group discussion. Unless you know the background each of them brings to the seminar, you can't make the most of the valuable experience you have at hand.

3. At the same time, it gives you the opportunity to "stroke" or provide recognition to participants—which is important to continuing motivation. "Edith, with your extensive experience in the use of on-line computers, you can surely add to our discussion of this point."

4. On the preventive side, this knowledge can help you avoid potential problems. If your favorite story on the barriers of communication involves a deaf-mute, you don't tell it if some member of the group is active in some non-profit organization that deals with such a handicap.

5. If you know the interests of the group, you will find it easier to capture their attention by appealing to those interests. Most of the men participants in my seminars follow professional sports, which makes it easy to capture their interest by referring to some recent, newsworthy sports happening: "I never thought Terry Bradshaw would ever pull *that* game out of the fire!"

There are a number of ways you can secure this information, in addition to the background information on each individual you should have secured before the seminar. At the outset of every program, you arrange for introductions. There are constant opportunities to get to know your participants as individuals during breaks and at meals together.

MOTIVATE YOUR PARTICIPANTS

The third guideline is to gain the favorable attention of your group and keep them positively motivated throughout the program. You have to do this or you can't succeed. If they are not listening with interest they won't understand; and if they haven't developed any inner commitment they won't apply what they've learned on the job.

You may confidently assume that you have a head start. "They wouldn't be sitting there in the room if they didn't want to learn," you may be saying to yourself. But don't fool yourself. You will be much better off if you make the opposite assumption—and you will probably be closer to the truth. Most of them didn't volunteer for the class. Their bosses told them to come. They may have heard some good reports about the seminar from past participants. At most they will be mildly interested and curious. But they may also be questioning whether they should have been more resourceful in getting excused from the seminar—or at least in getting a postponement.

You have to capture their attention and appeal to their needs—at the outset and repeatedly throughout the seminar. Note that there are two separate thoughts here. One is simply to get them to pay attention. The other is to gain their commitment and, if appropriate, a readiness to change their own behavior on the job.

Capturing Their Interest

If you stop to think of it, you have to capture their interest before you can win their commitment. If they aren't out there listening and interested, you don't have a chance of getting them to understand your subject matter. You have to keep the door to their minds open, so to speak. It usually isn't too difficult if you have matched the right people with the right seminar. But there are a number of useful and practical suggestions.

Get Participation. The best way to get your group interested is to get them involved personally. Break the group into teams and give them something interesting to talk about with each other. Virtually everyone gets a speaking part in such an exercise. A good deal of this is built into the seminar design, but you may well find further impromptu opportunities.

Suppose you run into an unusually apathetic group, which sometimes happens. The participants just sit there quietly. They may even smile. But they're not about to put themselves out. What do you do? Get them involved in a small team exercise. The worst thing you can do is to talk louder or faster. It is a little easier to deal with a fun-loving group. But you can easily be carried away by the fun and let the group get out of hand. Of course, to a point you *should* relax and enjoy it—but only to a point. You've got to get the group back to the subject matter at hand. Again, small team exercises can be a useful response. Or you can assign a case from the workbook.

Come Across—Personally. An important aspect of holding the participants' interest is to be an interesting person yourself, in your total impact on the group. It is difficult for seminar leaders to assess their own impact. Yet your total personality can have a considerable effect. Seminar leaders are all different people and shouldn't force themselves into a rigid mold. Nevertheless, our experience suggests three points to remember:

1. *Smile.* The first is to smile. Be relaxed and friendly. Your open, outgoing attitude will encourage the group to respond in the same way. More than simply a facial expression, you should exude an attitude of sincere enjoyment, treating each participant as a friend, joining in the fun, but at the same time being sincerely interested in the participants and in the seminar.

2. *Use Humor.* A ready wit and a light touch help to make the seminar a pleasant experience and provide occasional moments of mental relaxation. Sometimes you can tie humorous stories to specific points to be made in the seminar. If done well and not overdone, the technique can release tension and prevent boredom.

    I knew a seminar leader years ago who was so expert at getting laughs that his seminars were a continuous series of humorous asides and funny stories. The participants loved it. They would emerge from the seminar room each day with tears of laughter still twinkling in their eyes. But as a learning experience, it was a failure. Joke retention was high, but subject matter became secondary.

    Sometimes jokes can be offensive to people. Ethnic, racial, and sexist stories are, of course, to be avoided; they are simply in poor taste. But different individuals may have quite different views as to what is in "good taste" or "bad taste." What strikes one group as uproariously funny may impress another group as "coarse." A good rule is: when in doubt, don't tell it.

Nevertheless, humor has an important place. Plan your stories in advance and key them right into your notes. Use the reactions of different groups to your stories as a means of sorting them out. Keep the ones that always get a good laugh and illustrate a point and you will have little risk of offending anyone. Get rid of the others. This means you have to be on the alert to collect stories that could be used in your seminars to provide a change of pace and make a relevant impact on the group.

3. *Be Alive.* The true test of the professional is an ability to be keenly alive, even enthusiastic, though conducting the same program over and over again. Stop to think about it. If you act bored or placid, others will surely lose interest.

Be careful of your own non-verbal cues. Do you keep a lively eye-contact with individuals in the group? Do you stand up most of the time? Do you move around? Are you effusive in recognizing the useful contributions of individuals to the discussion? Do you consciously vary the tone and loudness of your voice? Or, on the other hand, are you seated most of the time? Leaning on your elbows? When you do walk, do you slouch with hands in pockets? It all adds up to your own personality impact.

Make Everything Relevant. Seminar participants have to see the relevance of the program to their own goals to awaken their interest and provide for continuing motivation. If they see its relevance they will become favorably motivated. They will get the impetus they need for going through the seminar process. If they can see a real pay-off for themselves, their motivation will be enhanced.

One special challenge here is that sometimes participants are already generally familiar with the subject matter of the course. Take, for example, my own experience in management training seminars. Many managers already know something about setting objectives, delegating, and other subjects covered in these seminars. They probably think they know a lot more than they actually do. The challenge, then, is to get them to realize that the seminar teaches a systematic, logical way of doing many things they are probably already doing, a way that has been thoroughly tested by many generations of successful managers "on the firing line." This is the pay-off: a short cut to improved effectiveness in getting results through others—a result that can be translated into a better chance for advancement and faster compensation progress.

For other types of training seminars, the pay-off may be even easier to find. "If you really learn and apply this step-by-step selling method, you'll be able to increase your sales effectiveness, revenue, *and* your annual bonus."

Selling the course to participants at the outset is critical; but it is also important to point out the relevance of each new idea as it comes along in the seminar. Everything you do must appear to be relevant to the participants.

Keep a Good Pace. If you keep the pace moving properly, with frequent changes of approach, it will help to keep the interest level high. It's not always easy. If you try to keep everyone productively learning, you may lose the fast learners who are likely to be the informal leaders in the group. If you cater too much to them, you may leave the slow learners behind. Your best bet probably is to steer a middle course, giving the fast learners opportunities to show off. If necessary, give the slower ones some after-hours coaching.

The rationale for changing the pace and method from time to time is to avoid boredom. Adults need mental rest periods to maintain a high involvement level. They need opportunities to move around physically to help avoid mental fatigue. What you want to hear from the participants are comments like these: "Boy, the morning sure passed quickly." "I wasn't looking forward to this seminar. My boss made me come. But now I'm really glad I'm here."

You cannot set and keep the right pace unless you are constantly alert to feedback from the group. You have to observe and react to many kinds of signals you'll get. A puzzled look is a clue to repeat, restate, or probe. A sudden gesture often announces the arrival of a good idea to a participant, suggesting the opportunity for a direct, open question. Watch out for frowns and head shakings; they are clues that you have disagreement. Get it out in the open or it's likely to fester. The same is true with side comments. If they're worth sharing with a neighbor, they need to be shared with the group.

Gaining Their Commitment

Getting the commitment of your participants becomes possible only after you have captured their interest. If you are working with a good seminar, the material itself will go a long way toward gaining the emotional commitment necessary for the participants to truly want to learn and to become eager to try their knowledge out on the job. But there are certain things you can do that will be an important help.

Provide Self-Satisfaction. Give your participants the satisfaction that comes from learning. Every time you pose a challenging question or make a work assignment you are, in fact, providing your participants with an opportunity to test their own understanding. If they pass the test to their—and your—satisfaction it has a positive motivational impact. The response is more positive to the extent they feel they have been truly challenged. If it was too easy, they won't get any satisfaction. In fact, you may get a negative impact.

Give Recognition. Closely related to creating self-satisfaction is to provide recognition to individual participants, when it is earned. The recognition that you give in the classroom can have a significant effect. Don't underrate your influence here. If you find the opportunity to tell some participant, in front of the whole class, that he or she did a fine job, it is really appreciated. It evokes a very positive emotional response.

But remember to be specific when you give out these "strokes." Simply making a general statement about a piece of "good work" does not have the same impact as when you make some very specific reference to something that was good, and explain to the class why it was so good. It is especially important to recognize good performance immediately after it occurs. It is still fresh in the participants' minds at that time and your power to provide reward will have the greatest impact. Specifying precisely why the recognition is being given also gives you an opportunity to do a little coaching.

Remove or Lessen Anxieties. Remember, too, to deal effectively with people's natural anxieties. There are a number of possible anxieties that participants may have that can interfere with their learning. Some may be afraid they will look bad in the class. Others may be worried that their poor performance will be reported back to their superiors. The way to deal with these anxieties is to let the participants know that you respect their expertise in their own fields. Show them this respect by your attitude as well as your words. Tell them the seminar is designed to help them use their experience more effectively. Make sure they understand there is no negative feedback to their superiors.

Anxieties can prevent participants from really getting involved in the seminar. Remember, you are after their emotional commitment as well as their intellectual understanding. You have to capture their attention, hold their continuing interest, and step-by-step build a sense of personal commitment if you are going to get them to put the teachings of the seminar to work on the job.

SECURE UNDERSTANDING

When you have the group properly motivated, you have cleared the way to get the subject matter of the seminar across to them. Here are some ways you can communicate ideas and information, together with some practical guidelines on each. Although each of these methods can be isolated for purposes of analysis, they will be carefully mixed together in a well-designed seminar.

Telling vs. Asking

Broadly speaking, there are two alternative approaches to securing the understanding of ideas and information by the participants. You can tell them, using a variety of methods. Or, through asking questions and providing cases, you can get them to come forward themselves with the ideas and information.

Using the Participants. The more powerful, but more time-consuming alternative, is to draw out the ideas and information from the participants themselves. A welcome change of pace, especially for more experienced groups, is getting the participants to think up ideas for themselves which fix the information more surely in their minds. "Teams one and three, will you draw upon your accumulated experience to develop the seven most prevalent sins in performance appraisals? And teams two and four, what in your view are the greatest potential benefits to be derived from doing an effective job of performance appraisal?"

"Can you give me some specific examples of how we can provide meaningful rewards to subordinates, other than monetary rewards, to enhance their motivation?" This question recently sparked a lively and productive discussion among a group of top-level state government administrators who went into the discussion thinking there was little that they could do to provide rewards to employees in light of Civil Service regulations. Drawing specific examples from the group, as in this illustration, is an effective way to get participants to assist in the communication process. Their examples are quite likely to be more impressive to the other participants than your own. The examples will appear to come more from the "real world."

Demonstrations can also be arranged within the participant group. Some years ago I had an experienced director of personnel in a public seminar. Partly to stimulate his interest, but primarily for the benefit of the group, I asked him to role play a performance counseling session in which I took the part of the subordinate and he the part of the manager. He did a superb job—and incidentally enjoyed the visibility—with the result that the participants got a much more dramatic idea of the process than I could otherwise convey to them by words alone.

The participants themselves should be used at many different times during the seminar to generate the ideas and information that becomes the subject matter for discussion and analysis. You can draw them out by asking questions, or by giving them exercises or cases to analyze in sub-groups or teams.

Leader Exposition. The less powerful, but less time-consuming alternative, is to present the ideas and information yourself. Direct leader exposition is particularly useful with less experienced groups. Typically, such a presentation involves some mixture of direct statement, visuals, demonstration, and examples.

Direct Statements. The direct statement is the most commonly used of all the different methods of leader exposition. The direct statement takes the least amount of time and is directly under the control of the seminar leader. You can carefully plan in advance exactly what words to use to make the clearest possible communication.

But having the leader introduce and explain the subject matter has its disadvantages, too. Sometimes complex ideas or abstract concepts are not easy to state clearly. If the leader talks too much, the others lose interest. A seminar, by its very name, requires a sharing of ideas and experience, which cannot be done if the seminar leader is too busy lecturing. Talking too fast has a special disadvantage. If the ideas are coming across too rapidly for some of the participants to grasp, the communication will fail in its purpose. In addition, fast talk is often accompanied by a lack of clarity. The leader hasn't had enough time to select the most appropriate words or think through the most logical thought sequence. On the other hand, speaking too slowly will produce boredom and mind wandering.

Despite these disadvantages and potential problems, the direct statement, often accompanied by a restatement or rephrasing, is by far the most commonly used teaching method. Used alone or in conjunction with other methods, the direct statement is an essential tool for providing ideas and information, for correcting mistakes, for answering questions, and for summarizing a seminar sequence before advancing to the next. For these reasons, some practical suggestions for making these statements as easily understandable as possible are worth considering.

1. *Use Simple Words.* Language can be a formidable barrier to understanding. Not just foreign languages; more frequently, it is

technical jargon which causes the problem. Some disciplines are worse than others, but it is easy to build into your vocabulary, quite unconsciously, phrases, words, or acronyms that mean a great deal to you, but may not communicate at all to others. Fortunately, this problem is more likely to appear in written rather than oral communications. But you need to be on constant guard. Make "dry-runs" or practice presentations and have your audience watch especially for opportunities to use simpler, more specific words.

2. *Communicate in Small Bites.* Beware of "overload." If you pack too many ideas or too much information in too short a space of time, you can't expect to get understanding. Instead, throw out one idea at a time. Provide an example. Contrast it with another idea. Only when you sense the understanding of the group—or test it through questions—should you move on.

3. *Build on Prior Information.* Proceed from what has already been understood and accepted to new material, relating it logically to the prior information. Often there is a natural order into which ideas will fall, like a step-by-step sequence of action steps.

4. *Go From the General to the Specific.* Provide some overview or perspective at the outset. Then get down to the details. It will be easier for people to grasp.

5. *Break up Complex Ideas.* A number of smaller, simpler ideas can be the best way to get people to understand some complex concept. You want to present something that is not so complex as to be confusing, nor so simple as to be obvious or boring.

6. *State and Restate.* If a few participants were lost on another thought when you first made a point, you need to give them another chance to catch on. Repetition also adds emphasis and contributes to retention of an idea. A summary of some sort is indispensible before moving from one subject to the next and is itself a form of repetition.

Visualizations. Visualizations have the great advantage of conveying the whole idea at one time. Verbal communications have to present a sequence of words to establish an idea. Not so with visuals. Furthermore, many people actually need to see what you are saying as well as to hear it. They need to hold on to the idea and reflect upon it, which visuals permit.

a. Using Prepared Visuals. In well-developed seminars, you are provided ahead of time with a variety of visual aids complete with directions on how to use them. If this is the case, you still need to know how to use them most effectively. Here are a few suggestions:

1. Let the visual speak for itself. Elaborate on it, but—as a general rule—don't read it word for word. There may be rare exceptions for special emphasis, but your participants can read—and read it faster to themselves than you can read it aloud. Don't insult their intelligence.

2. Talk to your audience, not to the screen. If you maintain eye contact with the participants they are encouraged to pay attention. You will also get the benefit of any non-verbal feedback or response to the visual. If you are projecting 35mm slides onto a screen behind your speaker's table, you can place a hand mirror on your table in such a position that you can see what is on the screen. Even though the image you see in the mirror is reversed, you can get necessary reassurance that the visual you are talking about is the one that is actually before the group.

3. Remember to keep the screen in view of everyone. Don't let your own body, an easel flip chart or anything else get in the way.

4. If necessary to do so, get a participant to dim the lights for you or turn a remote projector on or off. Ideally, the seminar room and layout should make this caution unnecessary. But if it has to be done, you are better off getting someone else to do it for you rather than interrupting the flow of proceedings by doing it yourself.

b. Using Flip Charts. Your flip chart, a large pad of paper, usually 30″ x 40″, on an easel, should be of great help to you, whether or not you have a complete set of prepared visuals. As an alternative, some presenters prefer to use acetate sheets (or a roll of acetate sheet) with an overhead projector on which they write with a special marker, projecting their writings on the large screen behind them. This alternative is especially good for larger groups and may make writing legibly somewhat easier. But it has one disadvantage over the flip chart: you can't tear off pages and hang them on the walls of the room.

There are a number of specific instances in which it is quite useful to write something down on the flip chart or blank acetate sheet:

1. Recording team exercise response. One is to record the responses of a sub-group to some work exercise or case. Their response is kept before the whole group long enough for others to reflect

upon, absorb, and comment on it. You can use a different-colored marker to indicate comments that are from another team to create a little friendly competition.

2. Providing special emphasis. Another use of the flip chart is to add importance to a statement made by a participant or by yourself. Writing it down gives the point special emphasis.

3. Preserving for later reference. A third use is to save ideas generated, say, in a group discussion for later reference. For example, it may be helpful to collect the group's thinking on the advantages or benefits of delegation, which can later be used in summarizing the subject.

4. Showing relationships. Sometimes it is useful to provide a visualization of certain relationships not provided for in the prepared visuals. It may be something you have planned for this particular group, or an idea that comes out of a question presented, or out of a group discussion.

5. Making work assignments. As a wise precaution, it is useful to write down as well as give orally individual or team exercises, especially evening assignments. Even if stated in participant workbooks, the assignment will be more surely understood and remembered if it is up there on the flip chart in writing for all to see.

Although extremely useful, flip charts can be used improperly. For one thing, don't write down too much. It takes time. Everything stops while you are writing. Furthermore, you'll be tempted to write quickly, which usually makes writing less legible. Use key words. Paraphrase your thoughts.

Another caution is to avoid putting everything in your own words. Try to use words provided by the participants, if you are capturing a team response or points derived from a group discussion. It's a good way to provide recognition to individual participants. If you put it in your own words, you are claiming some of the credit for yourself.

Finally, write large enough for everyone to see and clearly enough for everyone to read. After all, your objective is to communicate. If people can't see it or can't read it, you have failed in your purpose.

Make sure as well that you put a title above your writing, e.g., "Barriers to Planning." The title helps focus everyone's thinking. If anybody's mind has wandered, it can more easily get back into the stream of discussion.

Appropriate use of handwritten visuals will add greatly to the prepared visuals in gaining impact and total understanding. Visualizations, both impromptu and prepared, can communicate some ideas and relationships much more quickly and easily than words. They can provide an instant impact, where verbal explanations require a sequence of thought. Visual aids have to be considered an indispensible component of successful seminars.

Demonstration

Another method of communication, demonstration, is of special usefulness in teaching technical skills such as sales training or machine operations. Actually showing someone how to do something can be much more effective than telling them how. Just think how much easier it is to demonstrate how to use a can opener than it is to explain it in words. Demonstration is usually accompanied by direct statements for purposes of introduction, and audiovisual aids may be used as vehicles for the demonstration. The demonstration may dramatize incorrect behavior to be critiqued by the group, or the desired behavior to be emulated. Undesired behavior should not be demonstrated unless the desired behavior is also shown. To do otherwise would run the risk that only the dramatized, unwanted behavior is remembered.

Sales training programs are especially appropriate for videotape dramatizations. A sales call by its nature has a lot of human interest and suspense. Will the sales representative be successful in getting the prospect to reveal needs that his or her product will meet? What obstacles will the prospect throw up and how will the sales representative handle them? How well did the sales person identify and react to the attitudes exhibited by the prospect? The dramatization can offer more excitement than the average TV soap opera.

You may find demonstration opportunities in addition to the sequences incorporated into the seminar design. For example, you might assume the role of the manager providing on-the-job coaching to a subordinate. Such a demonstration can offer a high-impact change of pace to the seminar. Impromptu role playing can sometimes clear up a point of confusion or answer a question much more effectively than verbal explanation.

Examples

A fourth way that leaders communicate ideas and information is through the use of examples. The method is especially helpful in seminars teaching concepts and principles to be applied on the job. Many people have trouble thinking in conceptual terms. Unless they can see how a concept can be applied in a specific, familiar situation, they may be at a loss to understand it. Seminar leaders can make abstract ideas come alive through the adroit use of examples.

Despite their great usefulness, though, examples can pose some dangers and have their limitations. Sometimes the precise relationship between the idea and the example is not understood by everyone. With certain groups, the example you have built into your repertory appears too naive or too unrealistic to them. If it's an example you've borrowed from someone else, you may be embarrassed by aggressive cross-examination. If the example is contained in a funny story, the joke may overwhelm the intended message in the minds of the participants.

Clearly, the usefulness of examples far outweighs their disadvantages. But try to make them relevant, easily understood, and not too lengthy. Draw from your own experience, orienting your examples to the particular group at hand to the extent possible.

Examples, mixed with other methods, are useful both in leader exposition and in drawing information out of the participant group. Getting participants to provide examples is a good way to "get" participation. Participants will get a motivational boost by the opportunity to tell a few "war stories" about their own successes and accomplishments. By all means, make liberal use of examples.

ENSURE RETENTION

People tend to forget too easily; they have to be helped to remember what you want them to remember. No matter how effectively you have used all the available methods for securing understanding, you have to ensure retention. It is a truly sobering thought to realize how quickly people forget. I'm told that unless you do something to prevent it, your participants will forget 25% of what they have learned within twenty-four hours, and 85% in one week. It's an appalling thought.

What this means in conducting seminars is that you have to state and restate; you have to find opportunities to review, and opportunities to associate your subject matter with familiar ideas so as to fasten it on participants' memories.

Use Repetition

"Tell them what you are going to tell them (the introduction); then tell them (the main body of the communication); then tell them what you told them (the concluding summary)." This advice is age-old. You have heard it so many times before that stating it now is in itself a form of repetition to ensure the advice is remembered.

A proven technique used in a lot of seminars is "The Three Most Important Points." Participants are asked, as part of their evening assignment, to think through the subject matter covered during the day and select what they consider to be the three most important points. They are asked to be able to explain on the next morning why they thought each point was important. This forces them to review the material individually as an evening assignment. Then, the next morning, individual participants are asked to tell the group what their most important points were and why they believed they were so important. A discussion develops naturally that provides a second review of the material and helps the participants to remember it.

Another, less-structured form of repetition is simply to state an idea twice. State it with one set of words. Then rephrase it for an immediate repetition. Those whose minds were wandering on the first go-around will pick it up the second time around. Those who heard it the first time will benefit from the reinforcement.

"How would you describe this principle in your own words, Mildred?" is another form of repetition frequently and effectively used. The question also serves to test understanding (and may be a way to get Mildred to participate). If Mildred really can state the principle correctly, it will give her some satisfaction and give you the opportunity to provide a little recognition. Now, if you look back over this paragraph, you can see that some repetition was used here in references back to portions of the chapter on motivating participants.

Associate with Familiar Ideas

The other usual way to ensure retention, association, is the concept behind some well-known memory feats. Perhaps you have witnessed some performer recall correctly and in the exact sequence a long list of objects that had previously been stated. How? The performer has memorized a long list of verbs. As each object is mentioned, it is visually associated with each verb in sequence. The performer visualizes himself or herself, for example, shaking the lamp, kissing a desk, patting a clock, and so forth. The sequence of actions associated with each object provides clues leading to the feedback of all the objects in correct order.

You don't want to play this game in a seminar; but you can still use association. An association that I frequently use is to compare a manager who doesn't take time to plan with an old water-soaked log floating in a harbor. The log is at the complete mercy of wind, tide, wave and current with no control over its own destiny. So, too, a manager is at the complete mercy of events and conditions unless the manager attempts to influence his or her own destiny by planning.

GET FEEDBACK

A communication isn't complete without feedback. A face-to-face meeting or a telephone conversation that permits two-way conversation is much more effective than a memorandum or a letter. You get immediate feedback. You know immediately whether the receiver of your message has understood it in the same way that you intended.

Here is one exercise that is frequently used to get participants to experience the importance of feedback. One team member is asked to describe a somewhat complex diagram of equal-sided triangles to his or her teammates while they attempt to draw it from the description they are receiving. The first time the exercise is run, the team member describing the diagram stands with back to teammates who are not allowed to ask any questions. Then, the exercise is done a second time with a different diagram of equal difficulty. This time the group is allowed to ask questions and get answers. Needless to say, the participants do a much better job reproducing the diagram on the second try. With the help of feedback, the communication is far more successful.

There is another important reason to get feedback from the participant group: to test their understanding. Wholly apart from the give-and-take of ideas built into the seminar design or induced by the leader for motivational reasons, you have to take stock from time to time of the learning process. Both the seminar leader and the group benefit from this testing process. The leader learns how well the group is grasping the subject matter being presented, information necessary to deciding whether to keep going on the same subject or to move ahead. The participants are also given the opportunity to assess their own progress, which is quite important to achievement-oriented people. They either learn where they need to secure better understanding or improved skills, or they are given a kind of reward—the satisfaction of progress in their learning.

How To Do It

The simplest and most direct way to test understanding is through the use of questions: open questions to the group as a whole or, more usefully, questions directed at specific individuals. You can ask a direct question to test understanding of an idea, or you can pose a hypothetical situation and ask some participant a question which requires making use of the idea. If you get a successful, appropriate response, you know that the idea is understood. If not, you know that you've got to do something about it.

It's a good idea to develop your test questions in advance and put them right into your crib notes. In this way you can be sure that your questions are clear, directly relevant to the material you have just been presenting, and have a sensible answer. They should be important in terms of the subject matter and challenging enough to command the interest of the group. Try to avoid questions that are too difficult. You may have to end up answering them yourself. In that case the participant doesn't get the satisfaction of coming up with the right answer, and you run the risk of appearing to show off your superior knowledge, which may irritate the group.

It's all right for the group to know that your question is designed to test their understanding. But it should be asked in such a way that it doesn't threaten anyone. You should avoid the appearance of being personal or prying. Your question should force the participant to think, not just to remember something that was said earlier. The question should have a ready answer if the participant really understands the idea involved. If so, the correct answer will generate a feeling of gratification. Both the question and the answer should contribute to the learning of the group as a whole.

Generally speaking, there are two kinds of questions that you ask. One simply tests how well a participant understands some idea. The other is intended to find out if the participant knows how to use or apply the idea. Here is an example of the first type of question: "How would you define 'delegation' in your own words, Carolyn?" If the answer is "Delegation is what makes people think," you will have to keep up the line of questioning. For example, you might say, "Well, give me an example." What you are trying to do is test Carolyn's understanding, not her memory. If she can use her own words or translate the idea back into her own job, she understands it. However, if she cannot do this, she does not understand it.

Another way to test understanding is to ask "why" questions. For example, "Harold, why do we have to have standards of performance before effective performance appraisals can take place?" In this instance, you are asking Harold for the relationship between the two ideas. If he can explain it, he's got a good working understanding of the idea and its application. If not, you have to keep after him.

Here's another example: "Why would we want to put an objective in writing, Bill? Isn't that just paper work?" In this case you're trying to get at the reasoning behind the need for writing down objectives. If Bill can't explain the reason why, you might have to rephrase the question. If he still doesn't know the underlying reason, you can be sure he doesn't really grasp the idea.

Understanding can also be tested by asking a participant to differentiate between ideas. "What's the difference between performance appraisal under the leading function and performance evaluation under the controlling function?" In this case the participant has to understand both the definition of the idea and its relationship to other ideas. Again, if the participants cannot do this, they probably have not fully grasped the idea and certainly won't be able to use it effectively on the job.

The second kind of question tests understanding of *how* an idea can be used: "What practical benefits do you get out of becoming a better delegator, Nancy?" If she understands what you are trying to teach her about delegation, she'll give you some very specific reasons—such as freeing up her time to do more management work or getting more work done.

A more direct question of the same type is simply to ask a participant how to use some idea. For example, "How would you go about trying to get your subordinate to identify his or her own performance deficiencies, Paul?" If Paul can give you some specific thoughts on this that are acceptable, you can be sure he understands it.

Another way to test understanding of use or application is to describe a situation and how it was handled and then to ask, "What would be a better way of doing this?" In this type of question, you ask the participant to analyze what was done in relation to what might have been done. The answer should also tell you how well the idea is understood.

Sometimes you can use a more complex question for this purpose: "What is the reason that you want to secure understanding and acceptance in any delegation situation, Margaret, and how would you actually go about securing it if you were giving a project to one of your subordinates?"

These, then, are some specific illustrations of how you can go about getting feedback from the group. A lot of feedback is coming your way anyway in the course of carrying on the seminar, which in itself may be valuable in gauging the understanding of the group. But, in addition, from time to time you have to use test questions to make sure you are getting the understanding that is central to the purpose of the seminar.

When to Do It

You test understanding at frequent intervals but in different ways. You do so whenever you want to find out whether or not your participants have learned what you have taught. You will probably find yourself testing understanding several times during a morning and similarly in the afternoon. It may be quick, but at least you do take a reading.

Sometimes you can sense from the reaction of the group that they are having trouble understanding. If so, ask a few questions to find out. If they do understand, you move ahead. If not, you go back over the point again. You test whenever you think the learners haven't understood or you aren't sure whether they have or not.

Be sure to test understanding after presenting an idea that is particularly significant, or one that is essential to understanding the next step. The more important the idea, the more important it is that you know how well the participants understand it. If you assume that a critical idea has been grasped, and you build on that idea, you will be in trouble if it turns out that the idea hasn't been understood. You will have to go back over it later and clear up the confusion. It is better to find out that something is wrong at the time it happens, rather than later.

A good time to test understanding is when you complete one subject and are about to go ahead to the next. In this way, your testing acts as a summary. It helps you to close off one subject and make a natural bridge to the next.

Whom to Ask

Usually it is not too significant to whom you direct your question. Sometimes you'll have another purpose in mind that will determine whom you select. Perhaps you want to get a passive participant to get into the action. Perhaps you want to give someone a chance to perform successfully before the group for motivational purposes. You may be asking the question simply to get someone else to summarize material that you have been covering. If so, then you may want to ask somebody who will give you the best answer. But if your main purpose is to assess the group's understanding of some subject, you might want to ask someone you think is a slower learner. If that participant understands, the others probably do, too. But you do have to be careful not to keep picking on the same person. Give everybody a chance.

Sometimes you will see someone looking puzzled during the discussion. If so, direct your question to that person. If for some reason you want to avoid embarrassing that person, then call on someone else and see if this resolves the problem.

Directing your questions to named persons from time to time, whether for testing or other purposes, has a special benefit. It keeps everyone alert. Nobody knows who will be next. If you depend on volunteers to do the answering, the less assertive may never get a chance to participate.

Listening to the Answer

When you get a response to your question, you have to concentrate on the answer you are getting. It is easy to let your mind wander to the next subject that you have to introduce. But nothing is as discouraging to participants as to feel that you are not paying attention. It is a way of telling them their answer is unimportant. It is disrespectful and likely to create hostility.

You may think that listening is easy, but it is not. Many natural barriers prevent you from hearing correctly what someone says and understanding correctly what someone means. Sometimes you think you know what it is that Florence is going to say before she says it. So what you actually hear is what you think she was going to say, not what she really does say. Sometimes your own biases or attitudes get in the way. You tend to hear the things that you agree with and that are pleasant and not to hear the things with which you disagree. Similarly with people. You tend to pay a good deal less attention to someone whom you do not respect or like. You may not even be aware of all of your own biases. The point is, however, to try to overcome all these barriers and truly understand the intent of the individual who is trying to communicate with you.

One of the most important rules is simply to pay attention. Look at the person who is talking and try to concentrate on what he or she is saying. Watch for facial expressions and other non-verbal clues to true meaning. Above all, don't daydream. Don't be thinking of that telephone call you have to make during the next break.

If you should lose your concentration and not hear what someone said, don't be afraid to ask for a repeat. If you are not sure, a useful device is to restate what you think the individual said and see if you get a positive or negative response in return.

Most people don't realize this, but listening is as much a part of effective communicating as speaking. To be a good communicator, you have to get feedback from your group. Unless you get it, you cannot be sure that you are truly creating understanding.

Reacting to the Answer

Now you have to do something with the answer you listened to and understand. You have posed a good question and you have paid careful attention to the answer. What do you do next? It depends. If it is a reasonably acceptable answer and you sense that the group is ready to do so, you move on to the next subject. Other times you may have to make some kind of specific response.

Suppose that the answer you get is absolutely wrong. What do you do? The best approach is to rephrase the question and ask it again to make sure it has been understood. Repeating the question also gives a little more time for the participant to think. If you still get the wrong answer, pass the question on to somebody else.

What if the answer is unusually good? Here the best technique is to give your participant an opportunity to enjoy a little public recognition and satisfaction. Try to avoid rephrasing the answer or repeating it. It will have a greater effect on the other participants if you simply let it sink in as it was phrased. This is difficult to do. Your temptation will be to jump in and put it in precisely your own words.

Now, let us say you got a more-or-less correct answer but it was not particularly well-stated. Sometimes at this point the other participants will jump in and clear up the confusion. If not, probably the most useful thing to do is to restate the answer in your own words, sharpening it up as necessary. Be sure to give full credit for the answer. Make sure the participant involved doesn't think you are trying to take the credit yourself. But you have to be honest. The group will see through you if you give false praise.

As you deal with the answers you get to your test questions, you want to liberally award "strokes" if you can conscientiously do so. Misunderstandings and misconceptions have to be corrected. But, above all, be careful to treat your participants with respect and consideration. They are all good people, they are all your friends, and they are trying to learn from you. The way you treat them will have a major influence on their willingness to give you the feedback you need to ensure full understanding.

SECURE APPLICATION

The final guideline in conducting the seminar is to provide opportunities for the participants to apply their new knowledge to cases, work exercises, and role playing so they can build new skills and behavior patterns. Most of the value of actual application will take place on the job. But nevertheless, there is a great deal that can be accomplished in the seminar itself, where you can provide feedback and coaching assistance as the process of application takes place.

Work Exercises

Work exercises represent one way to simulate application in the seminar room. These exercises can be either assigned to individuals or to teams. Participants are required to apply the ideas presented in the seminar to a relatively simple situation. The exercises are ordinarily contained in the participant's workbooks, but may also be contained in handouts.

If there is a choice, use team exercises rather than individual work exercises. The latter bring a prolonged silence to the seminar room, which can cause a loss of pace and interest. Individual work exercises do have one potential advantage: they can be used to require each participant to make some specific relation between the seminar ideas and his or her own job situation. On the other hand, team exercises will take longer, but they do provide for interaction between and among different individuals, which is generally preferred by the participants.

The purpose of work exercises is to get participants to apply the ideas they have learned in a more or less ideal environment. There are no interruptions, no erroneous information, no particular pressures. The exercises are probably more useful in gaining an understanding of ideas than they are for recognizing opportunities in which the ideas could be used. Be sure to let the sub-groups resolve the problems in the workbook exercises themselves. Try to stay out of it—at least for a while.

Have each of the sub-groups elect a leader who will then report back to the full group. You critique their performance when they report back. You tell them what they did well and what they did wrong. Try to give as much credit as possible. Relate the lessons learned to on-the-job situations as well as you can. Remember, your job is to see that they learn everything they can from the work exercise that can be useful to them back on the job.

Role Playing

Another form of practice application is role playing, which can be highly structured or quite impromptu. Role plays are usually structured directly into the program design. Seminar leaders simply have to follow that design, which will differ for different programs. Sometimes individual participants are asked to perform before the whole class for a group critique. At other times, they make their skill demonstrations in small sub-groups in which they evaluate their own and each other's performance. The use of videotape playback equipment is becoming more and more widely used for these demonstrations because of the unique opportunity offered for self evaluation. The playback feature makes evaluations no longer dependent on remembering details of the performance. The role play can be re-created through "reruns."

Sometimes seminar leaders can very effectively improvise role plays. "John, let's say I am a prospective purchaser and you are a salesman trying to sell me some office equipment. You have sized me up as being a fairly dominant person. Show me how you would go about closing the sale." If John handles the situation properly, you know he has understood. You have also reinforced some learning with the other participants who observed the role playing.

Skill Demonstrations

In some types of seminars, participants can practice the skills they are supposed to be developing under the supervision of the seminar leader and get direct coaching assistance. The practice serves to test the current stage of their training progress as well as to provide actual application experience. Skill demonstrations are particularly useful in training seminars designed to develop specific technical skills, such as the operation of equipment, or the use of a new computer language.

The Critique

Once you have given participants the chance to apply what they have learned in some work exercise or through role playing, you have to provide some coaching assistance for them to get the most out of it. This need is especially strong if skill building is an important behavioral objective in the seminar or workshop. It is a particularly difficult part of the seminar leader's job because no one really enjoys constructive criticism. That is why it is wise to emphasize the reward for doing better rather than the specific deficiencies to be corrected.

Accentuate the Positive. The purpose of critiquing is positive. If you point out participants' weaknesses, it is so that they can improve. Your purpose is not to make people look stupid or to make yourself look smart. Nobody really enjoys being criticized. Therefore, you should make clear on the first day of your class that performance is going to be criticized and tell them why in positive terms.

Watch out for the relative weight of your negatives to your positives. You don't want to criticize so much that your negative comments outweigh the positive ones. Try to leave the participants with the feeling that they are in fact improving. Of course, your positive comments should be sincere.

Be Selective. In providing feedback, you want to focus on participants' most important opportunities for improvement to make these visible and help them recognize these points. Then you want to help them overcome these identified weaknesses. You cannot expect to create perfection. If you insist on mentioning every single thing that they did wrong, you can weaken their self-confidence and commitment. However, if a fundamental is not used properly, you must bring it to the attention of the participant.

In deciding what to comment upon and what to pass over, your rule of decision should be based upon the importance of the specific weakness to their performance on the job. By following this rule, the participants will learn that the points you are making are important to them. They learn that they should listen carefully to what you have to say and try to take advantage of it.

Get Help From the Participants. One way to make the critiquing job easier is to get help from the participants themselves. The least threatening way to critique is to ask the participants to evaluate their own performance. You can ask them directly what they would do differently if they were to do the assignment another time. If you've created a good seminar environment, you'll discover that people are not loathe to critique themselves. In the alternative, you can ask other participants what the performing participant did well and what improvements could be suggested. This indirect route is not always appropriate. Sometimes the point to be made is fairly obvious and needn't be belabored. You simply describe what was done wrong and how it could be corrected. In any event, it is your obligation as the seminar leader to endorse or overrule the self-criticisms or the comments of the group. In many cases you will find they will be tougher than you are.

In critiquing performance, try to keep a light touch. Remember that you are criticizing some individual's best effort, which makes most people feel uneasy. Using a little humor can help to put a person at ease and soften the impact of the criticism. Always remember: never use humor that will cause embarrassment to anyone. And don't overdo it, either. Otherwise you will be regarded as not taking the course very seriously and people will react accordingly.

Wholly apart from which approach to criticism you use, make sure the participants understand the reason why the right way is better and the wrong way was wrong. Participants have to be able to understand the underlying rationale if they are going to be able to use your ideas in many different situations.

People Are Different. Another point to remember in your critiques is that people are different. Some will quickly grasp the ideas you present and take an active part in group discussions. Others will be less able and less willing to do this. Some may be very sensitive to performing before a group of their peers. These differences will show up in their reaction to receiving criticism. Some people may take this in full stride. Others may feel unusually sensitive and threatened. With such a person, you are probably well advised to take it easy on them in class. It would be better to give some after-hours coaching to such an individual.

Give Them a Vision. If you are going to get your participants to continue to use the ideas you have been giving them, you will have to make them feel that somehow they will profit by doing so. It is up to you to help them see the benefits they will receive personally. If they understand all the things that you have taught them, if they can see how to use them on the job effectively, and if they truly feel some sense of personal benefit from using them, then you've got them. They will continue to use what you have taught them long after your seminar has been completed. This will be one of your great satisfactions as a seminar leader.

You have to provide them with a vision. They have to see some payoff or benefit in increased job satisfaction in some form. If your participants see that this is likely to happen, in whatever specific form they may visualize it, they will really want to improve their performance. They will be keenly interested in their own progress and improvement. What you have to do, then, is to help them see this in themselves. Sometimes you can provide specific illustrations of improved performance that you can feed back to the participants. Sometimes, at the end of the course, you can get participants themselves— perhaps in an unstructured group discussion—to evaluate and share their own improvement perceptions with other members of the group. Even better if you can get the participants to identify improvements in each other. But regardless of how it is done, it is of great importance that the participants emerge from your program with the conviction that the ideas are sound and really work and that they can benefit personally from putting them to work. The greatest satisfaction a seminar leader can get is carrying his or her participants through to this point of conviction and enthusiasm.

As the participants file out of your seminar room, you experience a feeling of gratification in a job well done. You knew the seminar thoroughly—its objectives and subject matter. You got to know this participant group and were able to make adjustments and relate to them well. You captured and kept their favorable attention. All of the various methods of communication were employed with professional skill to secure their understanding. With repetition and association with familiar ideas, you reinforced and ensured retention of the key ideas. You know from the feedback you received that the subject matter was truly understood. And finally, you gave them opportunities to apply their learning and get constructive feedback from you and the other participants. From all this, you can be sure that this group will demonstrate a significant improvement in productivity on the job. You have indeed presented a successful seminar.

Chapter 11

Post-Seminar Evaluation & Follow Up

The story of successful seminars reaches a climax with the stand-up round of applause for the seminar leader, but it doesn't end there. You still have to evaluate the seminar itself, motivate the participants to put their new learning to work on the job, and measure the impact of the training effort on changed behavior patterns and, if possible, on productivity. A good case can be made for the importance of this total post-seminar effort, but for many very practical reasons, most training directors rely almost exclusively on evaluations written up by the participants at the completion of the seminar, which they appropriately refer to as "smile sheets."

PARTICIPANT EVALUATIONS

The most generally used post-seminar evaluation takes place right in the seminar room. The participants are asked to fill out a form to give their opinions on the quality of the presentation and subject matter and the relevance of their new learning to their job responsibilities. There are differences of opinion on the reliability of these judgments. The main criticism voiced is that the participants may be unduly influenced by the pleasure of the experience rather than its value in terms of improved performance. This criticism is especially directed at evaluations made in the glow of the seminar leader's last impassioned summary. One training director flatly states he doesn't care what the participants say, so long as he can show a measurably improved performance on the job.

Why Do It

Despite these criticisms, participant evaluations can be helpful, if interpreted with good judgment in light of all the surrounding circumstances. Even if the performance of the presenter produces an upward bias, you still get a picture of the strongest and weakest portions of the program. The evaluations can be helpful to the presenter in improving future seminars. In some instances, the comments of participants can result in a redesign of the seminar.

Furthermore, patterns may emerge from one group to the next, if the seminar is a continuing one. For example, if the visual aids are consistently rated lower than other aspects of the seminar, you can reasonably conclude there is the need for improvement in the visuals. If your favorite cost-effective facility is always rated on the low side, you might want to get another place for your seminar. If a change in location is not practical, you might find it worthwhile for the presenter to mention the favorable economics of the site at an early point in the seminar.

The participants' "smile sheets" may also offer a motivational advantage. In this democratic country, "the voice of the people" has an important value. If some participant has a very strong reaction, either positive or negative, some tension can be created if there is no outlet through which to express it. And remember, all these participants are going back into your organization, influencing the total "climate." Some day they may be influential members of the higher management hierarchy.

How to Do It

In using participant evaluations, there are some guidelines that can be developed from accumulated experience. You may not agree with all of them, but perhaps they will start you thinking about the subject.

Develop a Standard Form. The first suggestion is to develop a standard form that is partly structured and partly unstructured. The structure makes it easy to make statistical summaries. The unstructured portion encourages creative contributions. We favor a rather simple form that focuses separately on the presentation, the subject matter and the overall impact of the seminar, while providing a few "open end" questions (see Fig. 12). You will note that our form features a

Figure 12
LOUIS A. ALLEN ASSOCIATES, INC.
CONFIDENTIAL PARTICIPANT EVALUATION

Program _____ Presenter _____ Dates _____

City _____ Public _____ In-Company _____

Presentation (Circle your answer)

Question		1	2	3	4	5	
1. How would you describe the presenter's knowledge of the subject matter?	Limited	1	2	3	4	5	Extensive
2. In general, how did the presenter treat differing viewpoints?	With Antagonism	1	2	3	4	5	Acknowledged them
3. How did you find the presenter's style of delivery?	Uninteresting	1	2	3	4	5	Dynamic
4. Were the concepts, principles and techniques explained in an understandable manner?	Seldom	1	2	3	4	5	Consistently
5. Did the presenter invite and encourage individual participation?	Seldom	1	2	3	4	5	Consistently
6. Did the presenter maintain control of the discussion and work groups?	Seldom	1	2	3	4	5	Consistently
7. Did the presenter use visual aids for reinforcement of discussion points?	Seldom	1	2	3	4	5	Consistently

8. Did the presenter hold your interest?

Seldom				Consistently
1	2	3	4	5

Program Content

9. Was the program content organized so that you could understand it?

Difficult to Understand				Easy to Understand
1	2	3	4	5

10. Did you find the workbook clearly outlined the content of the program?

Not very clear				Very clear
1	2	3	4	5

11. How often could you relate the situation in the case studies to your own job?

Seldom				Consistently
1	2	3	4	5

12. Did you find participation in the application exercises beneficial?

Seldom				Consistently
1	2	3	4	5

13. How useful did you find the visual aids used? (slides, Vu-graphs, etc.)

Of no use				Very Useful
1	2	3	4	5

Program Overall

14. Do you think that you will be able to apply what you learned in this program to your job situation?

Seldom				Consistently
1	2	3	4	5

15. Did you feel challenged by the content and the exercises?

Seldom				Consistently
1	2	3	4	5

16. To what degree did you feel that the content and exercises were relevant to your job?

Not relevant				Very relevant
1	2	3	4	5

Figure 12
LOUIS ALLEN ASSOCIATES, INC.
CONFIDENTIAL PARTICIPANT EVALUATION

Program _____ Presenter _____ Dates _____
City _____ Public _____ In-Company _____

17. How would you rate the facility in which the program was
held?

Poor				Exceptional
1	2	3	4	5

18. Please comment on any question (Presentation, Program Content or Program Overall) to which you gave a rating of 1 or 5.

Question
Number: Comments:

19. Do you have any additional comments regarding program or presentation strengths and weaknesses?

_____

_____

_____

_____

_____

Participant Profile. Your answers to the following questions are for our research purposes only. You may sign or not, as you wish.

A. Type of business or enterprise _____

B. Your position title _____ C. Years in management _____

D. Educational level _____ Signature _____

Form No. 640.1 (1/81)

five-point scale to provide a range of scoring options but without too much definition on the precise meaning of each. Our own experience would indicate that successful seminars will get at least 80% of the responses in the 4 and 5 categories.

Get Immediate Evaluations. Get the evaluations filled out before the participants leave the seminar room, even at the risk of a positive bias. Why? A simple answer: to get 100% response. If you try to get the responses at a later date, you may get only 60% to 70% and cannot be sure how truly representative they are. Members of the "silent majority" may not be fully represented. It takes time and effort to fill out the form—time and effort more likely to be expended by those with something particular they want to say. Often negative.

Encourage Signed Forms. Try to get the participants to sign their evaluations. But do it gently. You don't want to force them, if they prefer to remain anonymous. The reason for getting their signatures is to help in reviewing the evaluations. If, for example, you know that some individual participant was forced to go to the seminar against his or her will, you might expect a less favorable evaluation. Furthermore, you may value the judgment of some individuals more than others.

Use With Care. Participant evaluations are valuable, but after all, you are the professional in the training business. It is your professional judgment that should have the greatest weight.

Let me offer an illustration from recent experience. A management seminar specially designed for higher management levels had been getting excellent ratings from three prior groups when it suddenly was rated just satisfactory with a few strongly negative votes. Was it the presenter who had gone stale? Was it due to unusually poor timing (the participants were constantly on the telephone with their subordinates to finalize strategic plans that were due on the day after the seminar)? Was it the makeup of the group (there were two "angry young men" represented)? It was extraordinarily difficult to sort out these possibilities. Some changes were made in the seminar to step up the pace and to provide more team exercises on "real world" problems. With these changes, and a more sensitive eye on timing, the training director was pleased to see the "excellent" ratings will be resumed. If he had taken the evaluations at face value, he might have abandoned a seminar that had been having a positive impact with other groups.

MOTIVATING POST-SEMINAR IMPLEMENTATION

The "bottom line" is improved performance on the job. Many training directors realize there is a need to go further than participant evaluations of the seminar. There is a need to put in motion some specific efforts to induce participants to put their new knowledge to work on the job. In some instances it is relatively easy. If they were being specifically trained on new equipment or new procedures they are *required* by the organization to use their new skills on the job; no further effort is necessary. They simply have to put the training to use.

But if the participants are not compelled to use the new knowledge, it is much more difficult. They may sincerely want to, if the seminar has had a positive impact; but a backlog of paperwork has accumulated while they were at the seminar. Their superiors may be making certain demands that have to be given high priority. As time goes on the probability of self-implementation declines. For all these practical considerations, not to mention that old habits die hard, you have to consider the available means for "building a fire" under the participants.

Post-Seminar Assignments

One way to motivate your ex-participants is to set up an assignment for each participant to carry out after the seminar is completed. For example, let's say the seminar included training in holding effective performance counseling sessions. Then an appropriate assignment would be for each individual to use the newly learned method in the next performance counseling session that the participant is required to conduct, completing and forwarding a self-evaluation form provided for this purpose.

There are a variety of assignments that could be made. Participants could complete and forward self-evaluation forms as they next delegate a project to a subordinate, or next make a formal oral communication, or next analyze a problem for decision, or next make an important sales presentation.

Post-seminar assignments should ordinarily be developed by the participants themselves or at least have their understanding and acceptance for best results. Thus, if some participant has an organizational problem to face, then his or her project might be to apply the seminar-taught technique for organization improvement. Another participant might elect to use an action-planning process covered in the seminar to realize some specific cost improvement.

Reviewing the possibilities reveals one important implication: the training director has to provide for some way to follow up to collect the self-evaluations. An administrative requirement is imposed which has to be staffed by qualified people with the time available to do the follow up.

Superiors' Completion Certificates

Post-seminar assignments can be made more effective if a certificate from the participant's superior is substituted for or used in conjunction with the self-evaluation form, and if the certificate of completion of the course is awarded only after receiving the superior's certificate. We have used this technique with some success, the requirements for receiving the certificate being included at the end of each participant's workbook (see Fig. 13).

Figure 13
THE LOUIS A. ALLEN MANAGEMENT PROGRAM
Requirements for
THE PROFESSIONAL MANAGER CERTIFICATE OF COMPLETION

Managers who have participated in the Profession of Management Seminar may qualify for the Professional Manager Certificate of Completion, which attests to demonstrated achievement in professional management.

This certificate is awarded upon satisfactorily meeting the following requirements:

1. Completion of the prescribed Louis A. Allen Profession of Management Seminar.

2. Completion of the Management Work Assignment A, signed by your superior.

3. Completion of the Certificate Review Form B, signed by your superior.

4. Receipt of one copy of the completed Forms A and B, with attachments* to Ralph MacDonald, Louis A. Allen Associates, Inc., Palo Alto, California.

A distinctive vellum certificate will be awarded each successful applicant, certifying to his study, analysis, and practice of professional management.

Ralph MacDonald
Management Services

* Attachments will be treated with utmost confidence and returned to sender if so requested.

© Louis A. Allen Associates and reproduced with permission

The involvement of participants' superiors is particularly desirable. The superior is a much surer source of motivation than the training department. However, it does require cooperation from the participants' superiors, which may or may not be forthcoming. We abandoned the practice in our public seminars years ago for one simple reason: we had to depend on the participants to get their own superiors involved, which didn't happen often enough to warrant continuation of the practice.

Superiors' Orientation Sessions

Group sessions involving the superiors of participants are beginning to be used in influencing post-seminar behavior. One instance, reported by the New York Stock Exchange, involved a series of informal group sessions with the superiors of a group of supervisors who had gone through a time-management course. The participants' superiors there were given an understanding of the subject matter of the program and participated in informal group discussions on how they could help improve their subordinates' performance in managing their time.

Other Motivational Methods

Two other methods for post-seminar participation have come to light: one is publicity and the other is use of refresher courses. One management development firm used newsletters for this purpose. Performance improvement projects would be developed by each of the participants during the seminar. At the end of the seminar, the participants agreed to complete 45-day and 90-day progress reports on their projects which the firm would then use as the basis for developing a newsletter to be distributed back to all participants. The method proved to be administratively onerous and was abandoned, primarily because it required a great deal of telephone follow-up. Nevertheless, it might be more successful if administered internally by a training department.

Another publicity method is use of the organization's internal publication. For a period of many months, the Bank of America devoted a regular column in each issue of its internal newsletter to some management principle or concept. Each story was accompanied by enough specifics to make it newsworthy and give some individual recognition.

"Refresher" courses represent another approach to motivating participants to apply their seminar knowledge to their jobs. It adds a sense of importance and brings forward to their consciousness many of the ideas and information that may have been forgotten through misuse.

MEASURING PERFORMANCE IMPROVEMENT

If the final pay-off of your training program is improved performance on the job, how do you measure it? You need to be able to measure the impact of your seminars if you are going to evaluate your own performance as a trainer. Isn't this the rationale that we started with ten chapters ago? Namely, training is part of a broad-scale effort to improve the productivity of human resources.

Yet with a few outstanding exceptions, measuring performance improvement is not being done at all, or is not being done well. The reasons are very practical. For one thing, the methods for measurement are generally considered either too crude or too costly or both. For another, you have to be able to call upon the cooperation and efforts of the participants' supervisors, which is difficult to do in many organizations. In any event, considerable administrative support is required by the training function, which may have all it can do developing and conducting its higher priority programs.

Available Methods

The methods available, as one might expect, range from the highly sophisticated to the very crude. We have not attempted any exhaustive survey, but can report upon a fairly broad base of experience.

Internal Consultants. One extreme of sophistication is illustrated by the Fiduciary Group of Bankers Trust Company, as reported to us. In this organization, a highly sophisticated, computerized system has been developed that ties training directly into job requirements backed by standards of performance and productivity measures. A small cadre of qualified internal consultants analyzes performance deficiencies to identify training needs, and measures the impact on productivity of the training given. The provable gains in productivity are said to offset the cost of this staff by a large margin every year.

Control Groups. Another sophisticated approach* involves measuring productivity gains by groups going through the training against those not going through the training. Intellectually, this rather scientific approach would seem to offer the highest accuracy. But it has some practical disadvantages that perhaps explain why it does not have widespread use. The method is difficult to use—with scientific precision.

* Treadway C. Parker, "Statistical Methods for Measuring Training Results," *Training and Development Handbook,* edited by Robert L. Craig, McGraw-Hill Book Company, 1976.

You have to make sure, through matched pairs, that the control and non-control groups are as identical as possible. Then too, because of the difficulty, it is time consuming—hence costly. Some training directors worry about the reaction of those who are given no training in order to serve as control groups. And finally, the method would seem to be inapplicable to seminars that are not directly skill-building in purpose.

Measuring Specific Project Results. Sometimes you can measure specific cost savings or productivity improvements generated through action plans developed in the seminar and tracked after the seminar. One major city in the U.S.A. using this approach reported annual benefits of $9.7 million from twenty-three such projects and a one-time benefit of $1.3 million. Arguably, some of these savings might have been realized without the benefit of training in the action planning process used. But even if you discount the totals by 50%, it is still rather impressive. More importantly, follow up of specific projects is much easier to do for most training directors than either the control group or the internal consultant approaches.

Survey of Superiors. The American International Group makes effective use of a method that rests on a very sensible premise: that the immediate superiors of those going through training seminars are in the best position to assess the results of the training (see Fig. 14). Questionnaires of this kind structured interviews of the participants' superiors offer a good compromise between the most sophisticated and the crudest approaches to measuring the impact of training seminars on the job.

A prominent insurance brokerage concern, Johnson & Higgins, uses the participants' superiors in another way. It asks the supervisors of participants to identify their development needs *before* the seminar and then to assess their improved performance relative to these needs *after* the seminar.

Past-Participant Self Evaluation. Probably less effective, but still useful, is an approach that calls upon the participants themselves to make post-seminar evaluations of their own performance. It is personally less threatening than methods providing for the close involvement of their superiors. It is also easier to administer. On top of that, there may be a side-benefit: self-evaluation is a powerful source of motivation for self-improvement.

Informal Feedback. Despite all the other methods available, unstructured, informal feedback is by far the most prevalent method

Figure 14
EVALUATION FORM

Borough of Manhattan Community College
American International Group*

1. Have you noticed any change(s) in your employee's work performance since completion of the following course(s)

      Mathematics
      Language
      Grammar
      Office Skills

            YES _____   NO _____

   If so, describe these changes by checking off the appropriate statement(s)
      a. Improvement of skills _____
      b. Able to handle more responsibilities _____
      c. Shows initiative and creativity _____
      d. Is more aware of job expectation _____
      e. Is more effective in general _____

2. In your opinion, do you feel that this course was worthwhile?

            YES _____   NO _____
   COMMENTS:

   _____

   _____

   _____

   _____

   _____

   _____

* Used here with permission.

for evaluating results achieved through training seminars. Companies using this informal approach say it is one thing to consider the ideal "textbook" approach, and quite another to deal with the fast pace, constant change, staff shortages, and major unplanned interventions that represent the everyday world of the training director. Perhaps so. But this argument could have an element of excuse or self-deception as well.

It is a comfortable idea for a training director to consider the seminar completed when the seminar participants have left the seminar room: "After all, we do have the participant evaluations. As professionals in the field we can rely on ourselves to determine our training needs. We know a good seminar when we see one, to meet these needs. And with the evaluation of the participants themselves (fortified by an occasional personal visit) we have a way of reassuring ourselves on the quality of the seminar. All of these things added together have to give us a major impact on improving performance on the job. If they didn't, we would learn about it soon enough."

If any training directors should be tempted to rationalize a training function in these terms, we would ask them to reflect upon some fundamentals of management being taught, no doubt, to generations of managers in their own companies. What good is an objective if you really have no way to show that you have achieved it? How can you distinguish between acceptable and unacceptable results? Perhaps more importantly, in times of budgetary pressures, how are you going to prove the cost-effectiveness of your function? What evidence will you have to back up your budgetary requests for next year? Think about it.

Chapter 12

Recapitulation

You and I have come a long way together since you first picked up this book and began to read about putting on successful training seminars. Perhaps a useful way to think back over your journey is to ask this question: if you were to start up a training seminar program for an organization that had never had one, how would you go about it? It's a little unrealistic, but still a useful summary to think about the question in the abstract. The answer to the question can be structured around six steps.

ASSESS THE ORGANIZATIONAL CLIMATE

The first step would be to do some serious thinking about the environment in which you find yourself. What is the mission of this company? What are the major events and developments that mark its history? What is the nature of its competition? What is its product line? Its strengths and weaknesses? What are the directions and probably pace of future growth?

Within this broad frame of reference, you would then review the kind and quality of training in the past. Even if there were no formal function, people had to be trained. Was it all done on the job? Is there any record of success or failure in the past that would affect the overall receptivity to training?

You would also have to consider, as well as you could, the orientation of top management. You know that their funding support and their personal involvement can have a major impact on the scope and importance of the training function.

Also important, perhaps even more important when it comes to translating training into improved productivity, is that broad management population that may become the immediate supervisors of any given group of seminar participants. It is an amorphous group of changing population by its very definition. At the outset, you'll probably have to think of this group as the middle management group. You'll try to get some understanding of their value system—in particular, their view as to human resources and the training function.

You would go about this fact-finding mostly through interviews, legitimately passing yourself off as "needing to get acquainted." But you would probably have to supplement the interviews with any published articles about your organization or perhaps informational brochures developed for new employees. The net result would be to give you a feeling for the organizational climate, which you know has a major impact on the success of training activities.

ESTABLISH A BASE OF SUPPORT

This round of interviews will help you with step two: building a base of support. As you meet and talk to these managers, you would be alert for those you might be able to build into an informal network or, better still, a formalized advisory board or training committee. You know how helpful such a group can be in determining training needs, developing and getting approval of training plans, providing two-way channels of communication with user groups, and generally providing a useful source of counsel and advice. You cannot successfully function in a vacuum. You need to develop a source of advice and a base of support.

MAKE A NEEDS ANALYSIS

Your third step is to make a determination of training needs. Your needs analysis will become the basis for deciding what training programs to set in motion. You'll want to involve top management in your needs analysis, if you sense that it is feasible to do so. In any event, you'll want to work with your board of advisers or training committee. You'll probably decide to take a leading part yourself in the needs analysis, through questionnaire and follow-up interviews, because it gives you a further chance to get acquainted and build support. When you put it all together, you want to make an attractive, well organized presentation, using tables, charts, and graphs as appropriate to illustrate your findings and recommendations. After all, the first end product of your work will be to help create the image you want: a true professional who is thoroughly practical.

SURVEY VENDOR PROGRAMS

Once you have established your needs and have gotten them understood and accepted by the training committee and top management, you would see if there are good quality vendor programs available to meet some of your high priority needs. You know that if there are, you can make a much earlier impact than if you have to develop these programs yourself.

Here's what you would do. You would first telephone your friends in other companies to round out your own knowledge of what is available. You would solicit brochures and references from the reputable firms that could meet your needs, making sure to telephone their clients for a check on the quality of their programs and the overall service they provide. After reducing the possibilities to a relatively few, perhaps two or three, you would arrange a personal meeting for each side to learn more about the other. You would also request written proposals so that you could get a more specific look at cost and compare it with the cost and time delays of internal development. At the face-to-face meetings, with the outside consultant, you would try to gauge how effective they are in terms of personal impact and flexibility. Personality is particularly important if they are to provide the seminar leaders. You would involve the training committee in the final evaluation and decision: whether to use outside vendors at all and—if the answer is yes—which one.

ESTABLISH A SUCCESSFUL FIRST PROGRAM

The fifth step you'll take is to start a program; but make sure that the first program you sponsor is a winner. Whether you use outside consultants or develop the program yourself, there are a number of important points to consider to maximize the likelihood of success:

Seminar Design

In adapting or developing the seminar design, you'll make sure that the seminar objective and target group are clearly defined, that the subject matter is directly relevant to both, that the design incorporates a high level of participant involvement, and that it meets all professional training standards.

Pilot Program

You'll select a representative participant group and a suitable facility for conducting a pilot or test program. By running a pilot program first, you minimize the risk and open the door to program improvement. You want to be sure to select a seminar leader who is skilled in using all four methods of communication: direct statement, visualizations, examples, and demonstrations. You also want one who will be sensitive to the participant group, who will be able to capture their interest, and keep them motivated throughout the session.

Program Strengthening

No matter how outstanding the seminar leader is, you know that there are ways that even an "excellent" program can be made better. You'll want to incorporate the inputs of the presenter and the evaluations of the participants into this improved version.

Program Implementation

At this point, you would launch the full program. The enthusiastic evaluations of the participants in the pilot program should help you merchandise it. And continuing groups of satisfied participants should establish the program fully.

Evaluation

You would use participant evaluations plus a survey of participants' superiors to develop conclusions on the overall impact of the program. You'll try especially to get some measurement of improved productivity, even if this has to be a sampling. In the whole process, you would keep your training committee involved.

DEVELOP MULTI-YEAR PLAN

Only after this first success would you develop a multi-year training plan. If your management had asked you for this at the outset, you would have tried to meet their request soon after you had completed the needs analysis. But now that you have a highly visible success with your first program, you are in a much better position to get acceptance of your multi-year plan which you'll update every year. Even though you ask for funds covering only the first year of the plan, you want to start conditioning top management to the need for the programs you have pushed off into future years.

If you are able to take these six steps effectively, you have put to work the material in the first eleven chapters of this book. You are well on your way to make the training function in your new company a vital, successful force in helping your company continue to get better and more results from its human resources. You should yourself be feeling a great sense of personal satisfaction in your job—satisfaction in the demonstrable "bottom line" impact of your important work.

If training directors throughout our Western culture were similarly successful, the impact on our collective human productivity would have to be very substantial. The benefits would be reflected not only in greater job satisfaction for training staffs and their client populations. It would be traceable to a higher quality of life and standard of living for all.

Index

About the Author

LAWRENCE S. MUNSON obtained his undergraduate and law degrees from Harvard University and practiced law for over two years before moving into management consulting. He has spent over twenty-five years providing consulting services to various clients, mostly business organizations, and presently is vice president for Louis Allen Associates, a major management development firm. Sandwiched in the middle of this consulting career was a tour of five years in the "outside world" as president of a NYSE conglomerate and financial vice president of a $1.2 billion electric utility system. Mr. Munson, who is listed in *Who's Who in America*, lectures extensively and actively conducts management training seminars and workshops for many well-known companies.